My Roller Coaster Life Led Me to the Rock

A Spiritual Autobiography

By

Dr. Aretha Coleman-Terry

My Roller Coaster Life Led Me to the Rock

Copyright © 2021 by Dr. Aretha Coleman-Terry

Book and Cover design by Pamela D. Cox

Cover Photo by Cox Photography

ISBN: 978-1-7372225-0-7

First Edition

Scriptures are taken from the KING JAMES VERSION (KJV): KING JAMES VERSION, public domain.

Dedication

This book is dedicated to my Grandmother, Rosie Lee Mott, and my parents, George & Rosie Lee Coleman, who have gone on before me.

My Well Wishers
Pastor Elizabeth Humes
Pastor Don Coleman
Pastor Frederick G. Smith

My Cheerleaders
Dr. Alexis Gwin - Miller
Evangelist Verda Bowers
Lady Joanne Boyland

My Intercessor
Lady Tina Smith

My Family
Pastor Calvin & Evangelist Shirley Coleman
Elder Silesia Franklin & Deacon Willie Franklin
Pastor Don & Evangelist Sarah Coleman
Brother Danny & Marlise Coleman

My Beloved Godchildren sent from God
Trina Bohanner
Charles Durrett
Julius Williams
Keith Turks
Aretha Lae Yarbrough
Katrena Stone-Martin
Derrick Clark
LaQuonta Clark

My Godsends
Pamela D. Cox
Veronica Holmes

Table of Contents

Preface

My life had many ups and downs during my 35 years as a Mathematics teacher and a full-time minister. My experiences were like a roller coaster characterized by sudden and extreme changes that drove my emotions. There were times in my life when I was excited, exhilarated, and happy. Then, there were other times, when I experienced sadness, disappointment, and desperation. I was constantly walking with God, but I had a limp. God covered me with undying faith and a consistent prayer life. I was able to stand against the wiles of the devil.

As you read this book and peruse the testimonies, you will be cognizant of the fact that I stayed before God, not just during my suffering times, but even during the good times when I felt like I had it all together. Living a life of holiness involves walking with God and allowing Him to have full control of your life. My undying faith in God helped me to get through tough times in my career and personal life.

Living a life of holiness involves walking with God and allowing Him total control of our lives. God wants to play an integral part in every aspect of our lives, not just the spiritual. He is utterly concerned about our concerns. In Him, we live, move, and have our being. It is all about connecting with God in everything. He wants to be first priority in our lives, whether we are married or single.

Be diligent and watch God turn your life around.

Chapter 1

Walking with God is an Adventure

I was born on August 12, chapter 6 in Memphis, Tennessee. It was a Sunday. I have lived 22,439 days from the day I was born to this date. Oh, by the way, I taught math for 35 years. I love to calculate. My parents were George and Rosie Lee Coleman. Oops, how could I leave my other parent out, my mom's mom, who was my grandmother? She was known as the soldier, who my eldest brother, Daniel, named affectionately. She was an evangelist, church mother, missionary, and a very firm grandmother who helped to raise me and my other siblings. We were raised in her home along with my father and mother. Her name was Rosie Lee Mott. She was so strict, or so I thought, being a little elementary girl. Little did I know that I would grow up with so many of her ways and mannerisms toward children. Her help in raising me gave me good security in teaching over eight thousand students for 35 years. The things she would say when I was just a little girl, stayed on the front stage of my mind until I was grown. I would find myself quoting them to my students, year after year. She taught me how to say, "Yes and No, ma'am", "Yes and No, sir", "Excuse me" when passing in front of someone, "Thank you" when receiving something, and "May I," when asking for something. She also taught me to look the person in the eye when speaking to them and to stand up straight, and oh yes, I must tell you about these other two phenomenons. We could not go outside without permission, nor could we go into the refrigerator without permission. I know today's kids cannot fathom this. Most times parents do not know where their children are, and children can go in and out of the refrigerator countless times, knowing the same items are still in there. A lot of times, little kids climb into the refrigerator and leave the door open.

Everything my grandmother taught me was like giving me a goldmine. I see so many mishaps and mistakes people make because of their lack of knowledge, raising, and training. They had nothing to pattern after. Thank you, MaMa! Because of you, through God, I have had much success. I also appreciate the way you raised my mother, instilling values, etiquette, and above all, teaching her how to live holy through precept and examples. You also had a great influence on my father. Teaching him that "holiness is right" and the power of prayer, praying in the home, and going to prayer meetings weekly. He became a sanctified, fire and brimstone preacher. I thank God for my grandmother. Because of her, I was raised in a God-fearing home with what she instilled in us.

My father named his church, Prayer Tower. We had three strong God-fearing heads in my home: my grandmother, my father, and my mother. Somehow they all got along and respected each other until 1966. I was at Franklin Elementary when one of my family members checked us out of school early and gave us the sad, terrifying news that our home had caught on fire. We all moved out and stayed in the now nationally renowned motel, *The Lorraine Motel*. After our insurance ended, my grandmother stayed with one of our relatives, and my dad became the head of our home.

We moved into a rental property in the inner city. The property was located on top of a washerette. It was about three miles from our church and a mile and a half from the new school we would be attending. We were living in the county when we lived in my grandmother's home. This was a total culture shock coming from our quiet, sheltered neighborhood in the county. Children were much different in the inner city than what we were accustomed to. Children were louder. It was at my new elementary school in the 6th grade when I first heard a cuss word. Living in this neighborhood was also the first time I heard very loud, secular music, "*Which comes first, The Egg or the Hen.*" I would hear that every weekend from our very worldly neighbors. You can tell when the weekend would come, the neighbors would drink excessively and play loud music with crying and cussing. Times were changing, surroundings were changing, and life was changing unpredictably. My brother and I were a year apart. We saw, and we didn't see. We heard, and we didn't hear. We knew we were growing up, but not necessarily so. We were being exposed to reality and the world among school children. We had changed from one school system to another, from the quiet county life to a lively city life.

I had so much favor with my new 6th grade teacher. She sent for my grades from the county school, but they never sent them. My teacher knew I stood out more than the other students because I wore dresses every day, and I spoke very distinguishably. I always would say, "yes and no, ma'am, excuse me, and thank you," and I always smiled. Believe it or not, all of those mannerisms affected my intellect. Even though my grades were never sent to my new school, my teacher made me an inductee for the National Honor Society. I was happy and my mother was so proud. My mother bought me a white dress, white shoes, and stockings. However, I never felt like I was smart like the other inductees. My dress code, mannerism, smile, and personality took me further than any grade could do at that time. Now that I am older and looking back, it was the favor of God and His hand on me. My teacher even made me a safety patrol girl for the school, keeping order in the hallway, and putting boys on the left and girls on the right. I became a Girl Scout, and the principal really admired me, which made me very shy. He was a man, and I did not know what that meant at the time.

While we were living on top of the washerette, we had so much company from the church. We didn't know whether they were overly friendly or could not believe our living conditions. Our family was well thought of and respected. My brother had favor with one of his teachers, and she picked us up every morning and carried us to our old school since it was so close to the end of the school year. She took us to two different schools until May. My brother always had extraordinary favor upon his life, ever since he was a young lad in high school. He had the most favor of the male siblings, and I had the most favor of the female siblings. We finished the school year out. We lived on top of that washerette for one full school year.

Our neighbors had about seven or eight children. They were all very nice and friendly. The mother was a hard worker, but on the weekend, she would do a lot of drinking and play her music really loud. That was the straw that broke the camel's back. My mother told my father, "We got to move," and my parents started looking for a place to move to. She did not want us to be brought up in that environment, although our school and church were on the same street. We soon moved to another rental property. They found it at 1391 Humber, and we moved before school started back. By this time, I was in the 7th grade. That particular junior high school, along with another junior high school, housed students that were going to attend the big major high school in that area. So I went to that school for one semester. I was promoted to the 7th grade at the neighboring junior high school. Even though I had only attended that junior high school one semester, I had so much favor with my homeroom and math teacher, Mrs. Cleary; my English teacher, Mrs. Williams; my homeroom teacher, and history teacher, Mrs. Simons. It was because of the prayers over my head and that I did not look and dress like the other students. So I was always dressed up. They truly admired the way I dressed, which was very churchy, if you will. I wore my church clothes every day because that was all my parents could afford. I made very good grades, enabling me to transfer to my new junior high school.

Our new house was located on a really cool street. We could walk to and from school. One of our neighbors was very nice, quiet, and family-oriented. The daughter was a popular majorette, and the son was one of the top basketball players and in the band. We would often have other children from other streets come over to play foursquare in the street. Just when everything would be getting good and in full swing, my mother would look out and see children who were very experienced in worldly activities out there with us and would tell us to come in and have prayer. Now that I'm older, I realize what she was doing. My brother, Sam and I did not like it one bit at the time, because we wanted to fit in with everybody else. But as they say, "Mother Knows Best," and we would appreciate and understand it better by and by.

My teacher thought so much of me because I had such good manners, unlike my other classmates. My grandmother, mother, and father instilled that in me. I was chosen to be in the main school play and the Christmas program. I really blossomed at that school, from being sheltered all my elementary life with the church being my only recreation and outlet. It was all because of how my parents raised me in the home with prayer and Bible teaching. I did not appreciate it then, but I am reaping the benefits now in various ways. You will see it later.

When my dad bought a new car, the landlord went up on the rent tremendously. We only lived there for about a year and a half. This is when my mother and father realized they could own their own home. We finally received our first owned home during my 7th grade year at Mason Jr. High. My parents purchased this beautiful home with two bedrooms, beautiful hardwood floors, two shiny glass cup chandeliers, a big kitchen, one bathroom, a small den, a huge dining room, a walk-in pantry, a nice, neat front yard, and a huge backyard next to a doctor's office at 705 E. Mallory. This street was the main thoroughfare because it led to the interstate. Many of our friends, church people, and relatives had to pass by our house. My dad took pride in fixing it up and keeping it well-groomed and manicured. My dad was so happy about owning his first home. He enlarged his bedroom, added a fancy window to the front side and another side. He even added a picture window in the living room and enlarged the den by getting rid of the enclosed back porch. My dad had the beautiful white framed house bricked all the way around and made the porch to match the bricks. My mom and dad were so proud of their first purchased home. We were happy and proud too, even though my two sisters and I had to sleep together in a regular-sized bed. They slept at the top, and I slept at the foot in the center facing their feet. Our closet wasn't any longer than both of my arms stretched out. Again, we had one bathroom with six people residing there, but we were happy.

To get to school, I had to pass through Longview Heights, where Isaac Hayes, Harold Ford, David Porter, Pastor Smith of Greater Mount Moriah East, and so many well-renowned people lived. Those homes were so pretty on Laramie Street. The students at Mason Jr. High were a better class of children than Loyalty Jr. High. The students even dressed better coming out of their fine homes. I did not have the quality of clothes they wore to school, neither the shoes. But, I always got compliments on my God-given gifts, and for singing in the glee club. I had a very strong voice for backup, no solos. My self-esteem was elevated. I was selected to represent my class in the 8th grade Spelling Bee. I was the Spelling Bee champion for the whole school. I did not study, nor was I coached. God just blessed me to spell by phonetics and being a visual learner. I was in the paper for being the Spelling Bee champion, again that built my self-esteem. God, once again, smiled on me.

I was already participating in the Christmas programs at church and school. Later on, I was in the Thanksgiving, Christmas, and Black History programs. All of that participation gave me great exposure, allowing me to be comfortable standing and speaking in front of an audience and adults. My friends would say, "Aretha, I do not see how you can stand up there so boldly without being nervous or shamefaced." It was God, preparing me for my career in teaching and ministry in and outside of the church. My mother did not allow me to become a cheerleader, majorette, or be in the band, but I could always participate in the glee club and drama club. That made me popular and gave me self-worth. God already knew who I was and had great plans for my life. I never thought of being a teacher. I would always say I wanted to be an Executive Secretary and travel with my boss. I was sadly mistaken, unlearned, and just did not know any better. That is why it is so good to have praying parents. What would it have looked like traveling the country with a single or married man, handling business? It would have led to many other dark doors through him or some of his acquaintances. It looked so glamorous to me back in the '70s on TV. Those were the kinder and gentler days. You can go out of town with your boss and it can become the worst nightmare of your life. A lot of men lead different lives on the job and another life after hours. Some lead a different life just when they are in town. Thank God for shielding me from dangers seen and unseen.

The students at school would take field trips to the circus, plays, and field trips to Mammoth Cave National Park in Kentucky. They had money to take school day pictures, go to the sock hops, school football and basketball games, and everything for a child to look forward to while going to school. I would be on the sidelines smiling, casting a wishful eye. God would always give me friends who would never make me feel insecure by asking, "Why are you not going here or going there," or "are you going to get your school day pictures made," or "are you going to the circus or on the out-of-town school trip?" Or, "Aretha, how come you don't have a boyfriend?" God always connected me with the girls, whereas, I was the leader and the spokesperson.

Janet Billingsley was my first real schoolmate and friend. My family liked her, so that was a plus for me. She lived in another school district. I never felt the pressure of her saying, "Let's go to the movies," that would have been a no-no, or "Let's go to the mall," that would have been a no-no too, or "Do you want to come to my house over the weekend?" That would have been a super no-no because my parents did not know her parents or what kind of sisters and brothers she had. My mother was so very protective of my well-being, welfare, and where I was at all times, and who I was with. I survived my junior high school years with joy at Mason Jr. High with Janet Billingsley. She was and is a very nice and sweet young lady. She wasn't boy crazy or a fast girl. I never heard her curse a day in my life and we are both 64 years old. She was part of my destiny. We finished 9th grade together at Mason Jr. High. She lived a sheltered life as well, but not as sheltered as mine. We were best school friends, and we were good for each other.

The next year we would be entering high school at Southern High School, where I would meet up with all my old acquaintances from Loyalty Jr. High and all of the 9th graders from Mason Jr. High, and I would meet all kinds of juniors and seniors in my various classes. We were officially in high school, where we will be noticing boys, and boys will be noticing us: 10th-grade boys, 11th-grade boys, and above all, senior boys. Where do we go from here? We were so shy and overwhelmed because we saw and met so many cute boys. Yes, we did have butterfliesssss in our stomachs. Southern High School back in the '70s was a school of middle-class students and students like Janet and me, who just knew how to blend in. Even though Janet and I were not in the "in-crowd", I was still popular because I was in the glee club and drama club. I was known for my sparkling smile and for being shapely, although I never try to flaunt either one because no one at home ever made mention of it, so, therefore, I never saw that as an asset until I got to college.

Boys, Boys, Boys were really saying a lot of flattering things to me. It sounded good at school, but I already knew it was only going to be known at school. We were locked up in church on Sundays, Sunday nights, Tuesdays, and Thursday nights. Boys were not on the agenda and never were they going to be found in the Bible. I had a good name, and Janet Billingsley had a good name around the school.

This photo is of my best friend and I at the age of 15. We are still friends and neighbors today.

We passed to the 10th grade and advanced to juniors. We knew we were maturing, but it seems as if our parents did not know. I was a very sheltered girl, but I knew not to have a boyfriend at the same school because it caused so many problems with others liking him, trying to like who you like, rumors put out on you, and girls wanting to fight you over a guy. I knew that could never be named among me, with Elder George and Rosie Lee Coleman being my parents. I knew how to smile, and smile, and smile, but never ever give my phone number. I knew boys probably thought I was trying to play hard to get. They did not know that my parents did not have the big smile I wore. My parents' motto was, "get saved and seek the Lord." They were not for any foolishness, boyfriends, going to the movies, downtown sock hops, proms, homecoming dances, football games, basketball games, and no jamborees. All of that was unheard of. When my friends would ask me in the classroom if I would be attending any of these events, I'd always say, "No, I'm not going to the game or prom." I knew I would be locked up in the church with my parents and the old retirees. Oh, how we hated that life with a passion, but our parents "knew what was best."

I met Francine Davis and Deborah Johnson, who would also become lifelong friends along with Cheryl Macon. Francine was a very sweet girl that my parents approved of. She was a cheerleader, majorette, and a scraperette. Oh, how I wish I could have been one for just one month in my high school years. She was popular and pretty, but she loved me. Her father was an alcoholic, but her mother was so, so kind. Francine had so much freedom as opposed to my sheltered life, but she was not wild or fast, even though she had freedom like a college girl. She never made me feel insecure, intimidated, or old-fashioned. She always thought I had it going on because of my God-given assets and the fact that I had two stable parents who were church-oriented. She had everything that a student could have, but she had no stable home. She never knew when she would come home and find all of her clothes in the yard from her father being stone drunk. My parents loved her and took her in, fed her, and took her shopping with me. She even went to church with me. We went on to graduate together from Southern High in 1974.

But while there in high school, I was nominated Miss Charm and became the senior class chaplain. Both of which my parents approved of. I started dating this boy named Clancy Smith, who was a football athlete, had the best physique, and a winsome smile. Other girls liked him too, and he was dating them as well. I did not care one bit, for many reasons. I was not going to be intimate, and God knew, and everybody knew, I was not going to the prom with him. I was glad for every girl that wanted to be with him. He told Janet, "I was intimate with the other girls, but Aretha is who I want."

Finally, he finished and graduated from Southern High and went to Whisper University. That is when we really started to date. My parents approved of him, he cherished me and bought me all kinds of nice gifts. He became so possessive when I started at Whisper University. By this time, he was a sophomore, and I was a freshman. I noticed then that he was not my cup of tea. So, he went his way, and I went mine. It was not easy at all. I had growing pains.

I eventually started going with the man down the street from me. He was eight years older than me, and that was what I wanted and needed. My family liked him. He was respectful, mature, and knew how to act. I went with him until I got saved. His name was Rick Hayslett. I had a Damascus Road experience with him. I was doing my student teaching at Southside High, and I let one of my students, who worked with me at Kroger, leave school in my car to buy some things for a Christmas party. The young man had a wreck in my car. Instead of going directly to the store, he went to Baskerville High to pick up his girlfriend first and had a wreck going down Horn Lake. Rick Hayslett met me and said these words to me, "Aretha, it's something that you are not doing right for this to happen." The words pierced me so and spoke volume. It was like God himself.

Rick Hayslett and I kept on dating. But those words stayed on the table of my heart. He was with me throughout my graduation all the way until I accepted Jesus as my personal Savior. He prophesied it, unbeknownst to him, and I took heed and ended the relationship with him. He was so disappointed and let down. We were good for each other. But I chose Jesus over him and our relationship. He told me, "I hate that you are saved," and Fran told me she hated that I was saved. They knew I had a made-up mind and I was serious about my walk with the Lord. I was about to start my career in teaching. I needed the Lord every minute, hour, day, and week teaching math to over 150 students a day. What! 1st Corinthians 13:11 says, "When I was a child, I spoke as a child, I understood as a child, I thought like a child, but when I became a man, I put away childish things."

During my junior year in college, my best friend's sister said to major in education because you will always have a job. The Lord gave me a special love for numbers, so I had math and education as a major. I taught school for 35 years non-stop. That was an excellent and wonderful career, especially with God in my life, ordering my steps, giving me what schools to teach in, and strategically handpicking my students so I could teach them math and about God by precept and example. The subjects I taught in math were rigorous, but I looked forward to going to work every day. I truly loved the students that God chose for me when I first started teaching. I would be so sad when we were nearing a school holiday because I would miss my students so much while the other teachers would be asking, "When or What is the next holiday?"

I would do more than just teach math; I would be involved in other extra-curricular activities so it would break the monotony of teaching straight through the 180 days a year without any excitement or hobby. I did not have any biological children, but the children at school made me their mom and counselor. They looked forward to seeing me, and I looked forward to seeing them. The great blessing was I would get a new group every year and God saw fit that some of my students would take me three to five times depending on the different kinds of math I was teaching. A student could take Algebra I, Algebra II, Geometry, Statistics, Bridge Math, Advanced Math, and Pre-Calculus. I had one student follow me to four schools up to her senior year. God did that. It was not planned. It just happened. I always look at everything spiritually. That was definitely marvelous in my eyes. Another student followed me to three different schools from her 7th grade year to her 12th grade year. She was a very nice and smart young lady who really excelled in math. Right before her graduation, she brought me some beautiful earrings that I knew God had picked out because she never knew what I desired. She did not know what kind of earrings I had been searching for. That was definitely God working through her. Different students would sneak behind her back and whisper in my ear that she was gay. I do not know whether they told me that because they were jealous of her or they thought I would see her in a different light.

What people do not understand is that we are not supposed to hate the person, but only the sin. Romans 3:23 states, "For all have sinned and come short of the glory of God." As human beings, we judge sins as big and small and white and black. As I had begun to study the word in God's eyes, there are no little sins or big sins. Sin is sin in the eyes of God. In society, you will go to jail for stealing meat out of a store for your hungry kids just as a person will go to jail for killing someone. It is a crime either way it goes.

My parents' church was a very small congregation with limited finances. God always blessed our church to stay afloat, regardless of the membership, whether they were faithful in paying their tithes, offerings, and assessment. God was faithful, and He saw us through. My parents had a steady prayer life. They put God first in absolutely everything. They even put God first before each other. They knew God was a jealous God, and He said that they shalt have no other gods. "Thou shalt have no other gods before me." Exodus 20:3 "For I the Lord thy God am a jealous God." Exodus 20:5b "For thou shalt worship no other god for the Lord, whose name is Jealous, is a jealous God." Exodus 34:14 "For the Lord thy God is a consuming fire even a jealous God." Deuteronomy 4:24 My parents were living examples in living for Christ. Back then, I did not appreciate their living for God so profoundly. Their lifestyle and living for Christ have caused me to get as far as I have today. I am living for Christ, trusting Christ, and worshipping Christ because they did. It is really true that "children learn what they live." The Bible says, "Train up a child in the way he should go and when he is old he will not depart from it." Proverbs 22:6

My parents are all gone to glory, but I am still holding on to the legacy that was instilled in me. It has given me my own relationship with God daily. The things I would normally say and confer to my parents, I talk to God about them one on one as if he is a natural man. One thing with God, you can discuss everything with Him, and He will not share it with anyone. He will guide you and direct you. He will order your steps in His Word. God is keeping me because I cannot keep myself from the lust of the flesh, the lust of the eyes, and the pride of life. My mind is made up to do what the Word says to do. I am an instrument in God's hand, the vehicle that carries His Word, an ambassador for Him, and a living epistle. The Lord bought me and paid the price, and I belong to Him. All we need to do and say is, "Yes Lord," and everything will go better for us. We will be in His will and not ours. We can ask what we will, in Jesus' name, and it shall be given.

After graduation from college in April, I worked at City Hall. It was a very nice atmosphere, and I had finally entered into the real workforce. I was working among different genders, races, nationalities, and beliefs. They respected me from being fresh out of college. I knew that was not my destiny, but it was the road to lead me to my destiny...teaching. I worked at City Hall in the Insurance Department for Policies. God gave me favor, even though

I did not know that was what you called it. I just thought I was well-liked because I kept a smile on my face and was always complimentary. Those six months at City Hall helped me to make the final decision to become a teacher.

Chapter 2

God Was My Tour Guide on My Excursions

I started teaching accounting to high school adolescents. Some of those young guys had crushes on me, but that did not faze me. I was trying to learn how to become a good math teacher and a strong disciplinarian. The high school girls liked me. They wanted me as a personal sister that they could share their personal lives with, such as boyfriends, sex, mama and daughter drama at home, and graduation. I had just accepted the Lord as my personal Savior and was trying to build and have a relationship with God a few months before I started teaching. God knows I needed that, and I am so glad I did. I started that school year going on a 40 day fast. That was fasting all day from food and liquids until three o'clock. It was total abstinence. I saw God work for me, making the children respect me. I was only five years older than them, but they abided by my rules, and I was able to teach them without distraction.

I knew I had to be about my Father's business. I knew I had a calling on my life at 22 years old, teaching my first class at Baskerville High. The boys and girls loved me and I truly loved them. I kept on smiling, teaching math, and teaching the Word. "What, teaching the Word?" I carried my Bible to school every day. Sometimes I would be ashamed of the students catching me reading it because I was just a baby in salvation. Everything they would ask, I would always have a biblical answer because that is how my parents would have answered me. They raised me going by the Word. So actually, it was just part of my vocabulary. The students who I did not teach liked me as well, just based on what my students told them about me. The teachers, principals, and coaches were extremely nice to me. I really enjoyed my career, as well as my calling, which was unbeknownst to me. I did not know until maybe a decade or two later.

When Terry Jones, the assistant principal, got promoted to principal, he asked me to go to Hollins Jr. High with him. I did. That gave me even more experience. Those students were from all the center court projects. I had the best and the greatest disciplinarian principal in the world, Mr. Terry Jones, Sr. Those students taught me the real world: how to survive regardless of what you don't have. They were respectful, obeyed leadership, respected authority, and wanted to be somebody in life. Here, students were handpicked for me to build their self-esteem, prepare them for college, and teach them that going to college was not an option but a requirement to escape poverty. *How you start out is no indication of how you have to end.* I taught them how to appreciate math, but above all, I taught them about God.

Hollins Junior High School was the largest junior high school in the state of Tennessee. I told different people that when I left Hollins Junior High, I could teach anywhere in the United States. The students at that school were from seven to eight projects infested with drugs and prostitution. Come what may, God had already given me my marching orders. Whatever problems these students were encountering within the neighborhood, they brought it to school. Before we could teach, we had to spend a lot of time disciplining. They were experienced and exposed to everything imaginable. At that point, I knew to get on my knees during my lunch period and sometimes my planning period. God literally spoke to me and said these words, "I have heard thy prayer and thy supplication, that thou hast made before me. I have hallowed this house, which thou hast built, to put my name there for ever; and mine eyes and mine heart shall be there perpetually." The Lord spoke those words directly to me, "and mine eyes and mine heart shall be there perpetually (constantly)." I Kings 9:3

Nevertheless, God made those children subject to me. I taught them math and God. They taught me life, reality, and the fittest. The principal, Terry Jones, Sr., received another promotion to clean up Center Court. They sent him to Mathis High School, and I went there with him. As long as Terry Jones was my principal, I could discipline, teach, and preach without missing a beat. God opened up so many doors for me. I wrote a play and presented it to the community in North Memphis and South Memphis. I was over the student government and various organizations. I had a Charm Club teaching the girls etiquette, prayer, manners, and speech. I taught them about public speaking and how to dress to impress. That was the last year I would be teaching under his auspices. Those three years under his tutelage groomed me immensely for my career. I did not know God would send me back to the same school. That is why it is good to have a good name and to be respected. You never burn bridges, and I did not.

In 98% of the schools I taught in, I sponsored majorettes, step teams, Ladies Unlimited, Bible class after school, drama club, speech club, talent shows, student government, Mother's Day and Father's Day programs, Thanksgiving and Christmas programs, winter balls, proms, after-school concessions, field trips to Mexico, Florida, Texas, and above all, New York City. New York City had become my second home. I would visit there 2 to 3 times a year. I had become a tour guide for Manhattan, New York, and Harlem. I felt like I was on top of the world. I had many talents and gifts to expose my students to, other than teaching math and the Bible. I always had extraordinary favor with most of my principals. My gifts did make room for me and brought me before great men.

I left Mathis High and went to Smuckers High. It was an English as a Second Language (ESL) school, so the school climate and culture were very diverse. In my math class, I taught Hmongs, Laotians, Vietnamese, Europeans, Indians, Siamese, and Chinese students. It was like going on tour in other countries. These students were very appreciative of their education and truly cherished it. They were very humble and respective, unlike Americans, who took everything for granted. I was so glad to have them in my math class, because they taught me a little of their language and culture. During Black History Month, they were able to exhibit their talents. We enjoyed each other immensely.

I left there as a long-term sub and became a permanent

contracted teacher at Thomas Jefferson High School. Every well-known black person in prestigious arenas, like attorneys, pastors, principals, etc., graduated from Thomas Jefferson High. I started teaching there in February of '85. The school was a stakeholder for that community surrounded by inner-city projects. Those students were very worldly, exposed, and experienced to street life. I was a very young teacher raised in the church and sheltered. I never heard a "cuss word" until I was 12 years old. In today's society, kids are cussed out on the very day they are born. There is cussing on TV and in the music they hear. Those students would fight, cuss, and steal, but there was so much love there. I really can't explain it. I did not want to teach in a school like that as a sheltered, sanctified teacher. The Lord strategically put me there for a twofold purpose: so I could expose them to Him and the children could see Him in my life. The transition was very costly, but the rewards God gave me were out of this world. The Lord told me at lunchtime one day to get over in a corner and pray during my 30-minute break. I felt so awkward, but when I obeyed God, the children were like soldiers and robots. They were so afraid of "little ole me", but it was God and the power of prayer. Some of the students were afraid to come to my class, but they had to have my math class to graduate. They were stuck between a rock and a hard place. Some would stand outside my door and others would go to the principal and complain. He told them to get out of his office and go to my class. He told them he was glad to get someone to put them in check because they had run five other teachers away before I got there. The teacher, whose place I took, said there was no way I was going to make it through that semester. She said every day she would come to work, and she would get sick. The only thing that she would look forward to was payday and fried whole catfish on Fridays. She said she could not take it anymore. They could have the paycheck and Friday's catfish for teachers. When I heard that I was like the lion on the Wizard of Oz, I asked the Lord, "Why would you send me to a school surrounded by projects? The children are being raised by one parent, and most of them were young." Most of my high school girls were mothers already. I could have marched or run out of the school right behind her. I knew the Bible, and I knew God. I'm not saying that she didn't, but I understood that I must endure hardness as a good soldier. It is good to know God, and God knows you. That was my career, and that is where God wanted me to be, so I could take "my yoke upon me and learn of Him, for His yoke is easy and His burden is light."

Once I learned God, allowed Him to take full control of my life, and was completely sold out to Him, my career had become a piece of cake. I looked forward to going to work every day, all dressed up and made up. My job to me was like going to the White House. God put a prayer in my mouth and a halo over my head. One of the mothers at the church told me that when she looked at me she would see a halo over my head. I did not know what that meant then, but since I have retired, I looked it up in the dictionary, and it means: "a disk or circle shown surrounding or above the head of a saint or holy person to represent their holiness." I thank God thirty-some years later that I have learned the revelation of the statement, "a halo over my head." Another elder mother had joined our church and told me the Lord said I was his darling (his precious one). I found that in the Bible, in the book of Psalm 22:20 and Psalm 35:17.

"For I have kept the ways of the Lord, and have not wickedly departed from my God. For all his judgments were before me, and I did not put away his statutes from me. I was also upright, before him, and I kept myself from mine iniquity. Therefore, hath the Lord recompensed me according to my righteousness, according to the cleanness of my hands in his eyesight." Psalm 18:21-24

At this point, I realized many things: why I majored in math, why God made me a strong disciplinarian, and why I had a special love for teenagers. Well, as we all know, every child that is enrolled in a school has to take math every year until he or she graduates. Most schools would always have a math teacher shortage, and God knew that would be the norm. God would have me to transfer or go under a principal volunteer. If you transferred on your own, you will have to stay at that particular school for three years. If your principal would allow you to have a principal volunteer range, you can leave that particular school after one year. Well, I was very outgoing and had a whole lot to offer a school. I was a majorette and cheerleading sponsor. I did a lot of extracurricular activities. I was very marketable, and principals welcomed me. However, it was God all along. This is when I realized I was on a spiritual mission by way of teaching math. I got in tune with God and got on His schedule. During my 35 years of teaching, I taught at 15-20 schools. Some schools I went back and taught for a second time. That is why it is very important to have a good name. In five of those schools, I went back and taught math a second time. That meant my spiritual walk was not over and God had more work for me to do with a different set of students. I slowly recognized that my life was a living testimony, by showing love toward the unloved, building self-esteem, and helping students enroll in college or go to the service. I would teach students etiquette, charm, morals, and how to dress. My main priority was teaching and showing God through love and giving. Once I won the student's attention through those virtues, they felt comfortable asking me about my faith and beliefs. They had so many questions for me, and I was glad they asked. Sometimes the only Jesus the children would see was the Jesus in me. They were very unchurched, with three generations living in one home. The only times they would have access to God would be through my school programs honoring Mother's and Father's Day. They would write essays on, "Why my mother should be mother of the year and/or why my father should be father of the year?" Students were allowed to open every program with a prayer and scripture. After every program was over, students had the opportunity to discuss with me everything that was on the program from the opening prayer down to closing remarks. They would ask me my opinions and views on each piece, and that would be time to present and put Jesus on the scene. They would always ask me about church. They never saw a teacher wear dresses every day, always smiled, never cussed, and always talked about morals and etiquette. I thank God my light was shining in every school. He preplanned my career and my major. God would also let me know after three years, it was time to move. I knew He was in it because it felt like I was being promoted every time, although I would be teaching the same subject. The only thing that changed was the school, the drive back and forth to that school, and the principals and students. As a teacher, you will always have a new set of students every year.

My father was pastoring then, and we had a small congregation. We had come from a church that was a very nice size and family-oriented. At the large church, we had a big youth department and choir. We had all kinds of days that we celebrated. We, the young people, were very active and involved in the church. We would have holiday plays, programs, speeches, national youth trips, holy convocations, rallies, and annual days. I missed all that dearly when my father started his church because we did not have the large congregation, large youth department, nor the money to implement those different departments or Vacation Bible School. I missed that so much because I was raised in a large church. How many of you know that what concerns you concerns God as well? If you take care of God's business, He will take care of yours. "Delight yourself in the Lord and He will give you the desires of your heart." Psalm 37:4

At the school I taught in for nine years, I was able to implement many activities and festivities until I was satisfied. The principal was tickled pink. The parents were so happy to have all those things going on in their school. Many teachers would be in the back of the auditorium crying, and the students did not want to leave. They wanted me to teach them the next year. They wanted to go home with me. They wanted to hang out with me at the mall. They went to church with me. They would call me. When I got through with all the love and accolades from the school and community, a small church with a small congregation was all I needed. It kept me humbled, close to God, and with a heart of compassion for people from all walks of life.

When I left there, my principal handpicked a school for me. I was well-received. I was given so many privileges. I had a key to the concession stand, a key to the school's van, and a gas card. I felt like God had smiled on me. I started a Ladies Unlimited Club, which taught girls the Bible, etiquette, sisterhood, and hospitality. My goddaughter taught them how to step. It was like a high school sorority. Every time we would perform at other schools, talent shows, or radio shows, we would always land first place. My girls were able to purchase all kinds of uniforms and tuxedos. We won first place in every category. "To God Be the Glory." God did that for me.

Even in all that I was involved in, I never missed going to church unless I was out of town. I was very faithful to church and whatever would be going on in the church. I supported 100% with my time, talent, tithe, and offering. I never shirked any responsibility of the church, because I was so involved with the children at school and all the activities. Some sports would need a female chaperone for the girls' basketball team. They would always win their games and state championships. Whether they played in Nashville, Orlando, or New York, they would always make the headlines. It makes a difference when you are surrounded by a saint. They were excellent players and undefeated. I will not take that from them. So many of the teachers wanted to travel with the team, especially when they flew to New York. Those teachers would attend all the local games while I was attending church. If you put God first, God will put you first. Well, nevertheless, whenever the head coach got ready to travel, he would always ask me. My colleagues could not understand it because I was not a sports person. How many of you know that favor is not fair? The coach himself probably wondered why he always selected me, knowing I would come only to the Homecoming game. When God is for you, who could be against you? "What shall we then say to these things? If God be for us, who can be against us?" Romans 8:31 "Who shall lay any thing to the charge of God's elect? It is God that justifieth." Romans 8:33 God has always wrought many miracles in my life and career. He has always given me extraordinary favor, which was marvelous in my eyes. Further on in the book, I will give you several testimonies of my life that will not seem real to unbelievers. But with Christians, we know that all things are possible with God. "So shalt they find favor and good understanding in the sight of God and man." Proverbs 3:4 "For he that in these things serveth Christ is acceptable to God, and approved of men." Romans 14:18

I have always felt complete, even though my husband left me and I was a member of a mom and pop type church. My relationship with God, my parents' teachings, my self-esteem, and my students of 35 years, let me know that I was valuable to them and necessary to their lives. This always gave me self-worth and completion. I looked forward to going to work each day. When I first started teaching, about the first four years, I would dread the Thanksgiving Break, Christmas Break, and Spring Break when I was not carrying my students out of town. My students were like family to me. I always had a bond with them. I enjoyed eating lunch with my students more than eating with my colleagues. I knew I was not the ordinary teacher that you had in school. God made me different from normal teachers because my career intertwined with my ministry and I understood that. Therefore, I could not afford to be distant. God put out an attachment there, which was unusual.

Spring Break Escape with my students traveling across country.

Chapter 3

God Took Me Through, To Make Me Straight

I did not have any children of my own, and my husband left me early on in the marriage. We stayed married until his demise. We were married but not living together. God was in that. For anybody who was looking at me or even admiring me from afar, I kept my wedding ring on, which was very big and outstanding. That was a cover-up, and I could truthfully say, "I am married." Therefore, that kept the wolves away from me. God never let me discuss my husband, the good, the bad, or the ugly. Those who knew me knew my husband was a workaholic. He would open and close the company. God showed me how to carry myself, and I never had to apologize for my husband's behavior or actions. God had that "halo" over my head, making it seem like I had the ideal marriage.

Before he left, God had a missionary call the church's phone one Sunday. At this time, cell phones had not been invented. She was in

Denver, Colorado and I just happened to be the one to answer the phone at church. She said these words without asking for me or asking how I was doing. She said, "HUSH, HUSH, HUSH, don't you say nothing," and she repeated it. I will never forget those words or that phone call. She started speaking in tongues and praying for me. I asked her what this was about, and she said she did not know. She said that the Holy Ghost will reveal it to me. I told my mother, and she told me to wait for the manifestation. Shortly after, my husband left, and God let me know that is what that telephone message was about. I took heed and never spoke about what happened. I never tried to belittle him or put him down in any shape, form, or fashion. Pride can get in the way, but it was easy for me to "HUSH, HUSH," because I thought he was coming back. I remembered my mother telling me, "Never put your spouse down because you would have made up with each other, and people will not forget all the bad things you said about him, which you cannot take back or erase. People will hold on to the ugly you have said regardless of all the good he may have done or is doing. You would have been the one who destroyed him out of anger or hurt." Even though my husband left me for another woman (which was his mother), and he was a "mama's boy," he was still a gentle giant, kind, considerate, and very nice to all. He had a good name. He conducted himself well at home and away from home. I cannot say anything bad about him even though he left me. One good thing that happened to me by his leaving was, it caused me to get closer to God. "For thy Maker is thine husband; the Lord of hosts is His name; and thy Redeemer the Holy One of Israel; The God of the whole earth shall He be called." Isaiah 54:5

Since I have been walking with God these 40 years, I try to look at everything spiritually. "For in Him we live, and move, and have our being, as certain also of your own poets have said, For we are also His offspring." Acts 17:28 Nothing happens in life unless God allows it. "And He is before all things, and by Him all things consist." Colossians 1:17 That is why I can endure hardness as a good soldier. I know God seeth and careth for me. He knows how much I can take, and my steps are ordered by Him. Surely goodness and mercy shall follow me all the days of my life. We know that God's mercy endureth forever and forever. Our lives are already predestined. Only God can set the limits. That is why it is important to obey Him, keep His commandments, and have a day-to-day personal relationship with Him.

Right now, as I am writing this book, there is a worldwide pandemic called Coronavirus – COVID 19, where God is speaking full volume. But many, many people who do not know Him or have a relationship with Him, cannot see or hear Him. They are so busy, overly buying groceries and essentials that will last them six months. They are acting like a country that has been told that a famine is coming. Grocery stores cannot keep the grocery shelves stocked or filled. Those who have a personal relationship with God do not sorrow like the world. We know the words of Psalm 91, "He that dwelleth in the secret place of the most High shall abide under the shadow of the Almighty. I will say of the LORD, He is my refuge and my fortress: my God; in Him will I trust. Surely He shall deliver thee from the snare of the fowler, and from the noisome pestilence. He shall cover thee with His feathers, and under His wings shalt thou trust: His truth shall be thy shield and buckler. Thou shalt not be afraid for the terror by night; nor for the arrow that flieth by day; Nor for the pestilence that walketh in darkness; nor for the destruction that wasteth at noonday. A thousand shall fall at thy side, and ten thousand at thy right hand; but it shall not come nigh thee. Only with thine eyes shalt thou behold and see the reward of the wicked. Because thou hast made the LORD, which is my refuge, even the most High, thy habitation; There shall no evil befall thee, neither shall any plague come nigh thy dwelling. For he shall give his angels charge over thee, to keep thee in all thy ways. Thou shalt tread upon the lion and adder: the young lion and the dragon shalt thou trample under feet. Because He hath set His love upon me, therefore will I deliver Him: I will set Him on high, because He hath known my name. He shall call upon me, and I will answer Him: I will be with Him in trouble; I will deliver Him, and honour Him. With long life will I satisfy Him, and shew Him my salvation."

As I've said before, it is to our benefit and privilege to have a day-to-day relationship with God. It causes us to strengthen our relationship and increase our faith. The more you know, the more you grow. Reading His Word daily becomes a necessity as well as essential. God speaks to us through His Word. You can be battling a storm, need some answers or directions toward something, and God will address that situation through His Word. If there is a need in your life, the answers are in the books of Genesis to Revelation. That is the number one and best-selling book on Earth. It will forever be, and God just gave me this revelation. Why? Because the first four words in the Bible are, "In the beginning God." Genesis 1:1 The last words of the Bible are, "The grace of our Lord Jesus Christ be with you all. Amen." Revelation 22:21 As long as man is on Earth, God's grace will abide. The only thing on this Earth that will forever stand is God's Word, because He is the Word. Everybody wants to be affiliated and associated with a Winner, so God is. "Henceforth, I call you not servants, for the servants, knoweth not what his Lord doeth, but I have called you friends, for all things that I have heard of my Father, I have made known unto you." John 15:15

God always creates ways to prove Himself strong on our behalf. God knows that the only Jesus some people will see is the Jesus in me. That is why the scripture says, "Let your light shine before men that they may see your good works, and glorify your Father which is in heaven." Matthew 5:16 God sets us up to be on display because pride sets in, and God hates pride. That is the first thing of the six things that the Lord hates, "a proud look." "These six things doth the Lord hate: yea, seven are an abomination unto him: A proud look, a lying tongue, and hands that shed innocent blood, An heart that deviseth wicked imaginations, feet that be swift in running to mischief, A false witness that speaketh lies, and he that soweth discord among brethren." Proverbs 6:16-19 God always wants someone He can testify for and through, as He did for Job in the Bible. "And the Lord said unto Satan, Hast thou considered my servant Job, that there is none like him on earth, a perfect man, and an upright man, one that feareth God and escheweth evil?" Job 1:8

When my husband left me, I did feel like I could accomplish so much more in my life with his finances added to the pot rather than taken away from the income. Nevertheless, it was just a test tailor-made for me. God blessed me with more with my income only. I moved to an oversized condominium on the river and purchased a new Cadillac and a new Nissan Juke to run around in. I traveled more than ever. God was letting me know it was not my husband and his income, but it was all God. I had the F.A.I.T.H. (For All I Trust Him). I just had to trust God and watch Him work. I can truthfully say and write that God gave me more than any man would have dreamed to give me. No earthly man can outdo or outgive God no matter how he tries. God really spoiled me. I know that I am supposed to bless others, some I know in my circle and some people I do not know, so God can get the Glory. I can say the more I give out, the more God puts back in my hand. God has blessed me with the gift to give. My giving is so enormous, sometimes I have to curtail it. "Distributing to the necessity of saints, given to hospitality." Romans 12:13 God gave His only begotten Son, which means He gave His very best, and we are to do the same at all times. All giving does not have to be money. We give through our time, talents, and treasure. Make sure it is your very best. When you give, give the best of your service, and God will pay you for whatever is right. I have shared many things, from my mink coats all the way down to my diamond rings. I realized that when God blessed me with those luxuries, it all belongs to Him. I was just given stewardship over those things. I feel the world would be a better place if people did not have the fever of "me, myself, and I" or "my four and no more." Everyone needs to remember that whatever we have belongs to God.

During my 35 years of teaching, I found all kinds of ways to reward my students with money, popular t-shirts, candy, and gifts. When our school would have special programs where they had to pay, such as talent shows or field trips, I would let the less fortunate run errands, grade papers, or put up bulletin boards, so they could not recognize that I knew they were less fortunate. A lot of times, they would take the money and use it for other things, and I would be so happy that I was able to bring joy to someone less fortunate financially. A lot of times students would need personal hygiene products. I kept that available. Most times, students would tell me they had a friend who needed it. I knew it was for them, so I would issue it to them discreetly. I was so glad to be a teacher. I was always able to give solace to those who felt helpless or felt their parents did not understand. They would always look forward to coming to my class and seeing me. That also made learning math easier on the days my students would have doctor and dental appointments. They would come back to school and check in, just to be in my class. I am glad I had that influence on my students, knowing that learning math was not an easy subject for the average student. My students would always tell me, "You made learning math easy," "I hated math until I took it from you," or "I did not know learning math could be fun." I knew it was God that did that for me and them. Some of my students would go on to say, "You are the best math teacher I ever had." I knew that it was God that endorsed me and graced me for teaching. God put His signature on me, and I wore it humbly. It was not my math background or my education because all the other teachers had the same thing. "For He hath done marvelous things, His right hand and his Holy arm, hath gotten Him the victory." Psalm 98-1b.

National Teacher's Appreciation Day!

My career was a full-time ministry. I thought I attended college to become a teacher, and I did, but that was for me to get my foot in the door to do ministry. I really didn't notice it until after my first ten years of teaching. All the pieces of the puzzle just fell in place, and it was very comfortable for me. I enjoyed it immensely, and it felt natural. God was in it every step of the way. I would tell my students each year, "You were picked out by God to be under my auspices and tutelage." Those students were assigned to me. Some students I would have two and three years, depending on what kind of math they were taking. I knew that was God also. Ever now and then, I would have one or two students who did not need my math. They would take it anyway. I knew that was God. I had one student who was in the 12th grade and more advanced. She had several open periods, and she wanted to take my class, but my class was full. Her mother wrote a letter to the principal and requested that her daughter be accommodated since this was her last year. The principal made accommodations for her, and she became my aide. She sat in the class and learned and even graded papers and ran errands. I knew all that was God. That was not a coincidence. God knows how to send out a two-fold blessing. I have had so many miracles happen to me. I knew it was no one but God, smiling on me. As long as I promoted God and lived the life I was preaching about, God promoted and blessed me. The students knew that the male teachers, coaches, and principals had their eyes on me, and I knew it too. I knew I was forbidden fruit. I did not belong to myself. I am human; therefore, I was flattered, but I also know the Word. "What know ye not that your body is the temple of the Holy Ghost, which is in you, which ye have of God, and ye are not your own. For ye are bought with a price, therefore, glorify God in your body and in your spirit, which are God's" 1 Corinthians 6:19-20

I know my soul and body belong to Christ. I cannot join this body to any man that asks for it or any man that I desire to give it to. I am God's property. His Son shed his blood for my body. He bought it and paid the price. I cannot give away anything in life that does not belong to me, be it natural or spiritual. It's my body, but I just have stewardship over it. Anytime you are forbidden fruit, Satan will use all kinds of tactics, schemes, and cunning ways to trap you. That is why it is so important to commune and have a relationship with God. He will rebuke the snare of the fowler. David said over in Psalm 25:15, "Mine eyes are ever toward the Lord, for he shall pluck my feet out of the net." We are going to be tempted because Jesus was tempted after coming off a 40 day fast. "Then was Jesus led up of the Spirit into the wilderness to be tempted of the devil. And when he had fasted forty days and forty nights, he was afterward an hungred. Matthew 4:1-2 "He shall give his angels charge concerning thee, and in their hands they shall bear thee up, lest at any time they dash thy foot against a stone." Matthew 4:6b

One year I worked at a particular school, and at the close of the school year, the principal walked up to me and said, "Girl, I am so proud of you." I assumed he was talking about how well I disciplined the students. He said, "I am so proud of you because all these coaches and male teachers betted on which one of them would have the opportunity to date you." Little did he know, I was not interested in any of the 12. First of all, I had a great Father who endorsed me. He taught me about life, men, using common sense and judgement. He was the first man in my life that made me feel good about myself. He helped to build my self-esteem and self-worth. He taught me how to be self-supportive and not to depend on a man to make me happy.

My dad always said, "These men out here do not want to do anything but have a whole house full of children by you and leave you." He said, "You can never get ahead with a house full of children. One loaf of bread is gone in one day." I had sense enough not to go with anyone that attended the same school I went to. It would cause a lot of problems while you're dating, and others will want what you have. That would also cause a lot of problems when you break up because it brings about competition. Sometimes you may have officially broken up but not in your heart, and he is sneaking and calling you, even though he has a new girlfriend. It leads from one lie to another, and sometimes maybe a physical altercation. That has never been me or my nature, plus my mother taught me better. When you are dating in high school, a lot of your business gets out, and people make up things about you. I would see and hear that all the time. I knew I did not want to be in that rat race. I only had male church friends, and I had limitations to that. My main priority was to go to college, get a career, make my own money, and be self-supportive. I did just that, through God and by God, with my parents praying for me every step of the way. I felt so good. I passed that test. It is so funny to me, 40 years later, because I was the new kid on the block, but I had no interest whatsoever. I gave up my boyfriend when I started walking with the Lord. I was totally *"Souled Out"* to the Lord. The words of that song by Hezekiah Walker were my sentiments.

My students were very protective of me, as though I were their mom. I remember from the Bible when Moses said, "Choosing rather to suffer affliction with the people of God, than to enjoy the pleasures of sin for a season." Hebrew 11:25 The Bible already tells us to look beyond the present scene. "For our light affliction, which is but for a moment, worketh for us a far more exceeding and eternal weight of glory; While we look not at the things which are seen, but at the things which are not seen: for the things which are seen are temporal; but the things which are not seen are eternal." 2 Corinthians 4:17-18

Different ones would call me naïve. I just played naïve because I did not want to be bothered with them, their folly, or their foolishness. I would not comment on whatever they would talk about. I would just smile because we were not on the same plane. They did not walk the walk, nor talk the talk I exhibited. My response to them would always a smile. My peers would be so amazed when they passed my room. I kept my door open, and they would see how orderly my class was and how respectful the students were. There was no walking or talking without my permission, and students were busy working. I did not get that overnight. Neither was it like that from the beginning. It took a lot of praying, fasting, seeking God diligently, and getting up early in the morning to pray before I went to work. I am not talking about no popcorn prayer. I am talking about thirty minutes to an hour. It kept my children obedient and my mind stayed on God. I was able to stand against the wiles of the devil (those 12 male colleagues who betted they would have the opportunity to date me.) "Stand therefore, having girded your waist with truth, having put on the breastplate of righteousness, and having shod your feet with the preparation of the gospel of peace; above all, taking the shield of faith with which you will be able to quench all the fiery darts of the wicked one. And take the helmet of salvation, and the sword of the Spirit, which is the word of God." Ephesians 6:14-17

When we are on God's side, we are assured our enemies will be met with the irresistible power of His spirit. The spirit of the Lord shall lift up a banner against Satan and his imps. When my principal told me that, I felt so good, knowing that I passed the test, even though I was totally aloof to the situation. The young men were nice to me, but I did not see one that was my type out of any of those 12. I thank God for anointing my eyes with eyesalve. "And anoint thine eyes with eyesalve that thou mayest see." Revelation

3:18d I found out if you mean business with God and want to be kept, God will keep you, cover you, and protect you in Jesus' name. We also have angels that encampeth around us. "The angel of the Lord encampeth round about them that fear him and delivereth him." Psalm 34:7 "For he shall give his angels charge over thee to keep thee in all thy ways. They shall bear thee up in their hands, lest thy dash thy foot against a stone." Psalm 91:11-12

So it seems as if we believers have more than one angel assigned to us. In Psalm 91 verses 11 and 12, "his angels charge over thee." Angels is more than one, and then it says, "They shall bear thee up." They also mean more than one. Dr. Billy Graham, observing the plurals in both texts, concluded that each believer must have at least two angels assigned to us for protection. Psalm 91:4 speaks of God covering us, "with his feathers" and mentions that we are, "under his wings." Dr. Graham said God has no feathers or wings, and some have suggested that these feathers and wings speak of our guardian angels' wings, which cover us to keep us from falling, getting lost, or stumbling into unknown dangers. Now, I know we have keeping power if we want to be kept, and we definitely have our paraclete who is a keeper and a comforter. We are all human. We all have desires, but we have to bring ourselves under subjection to God and the Holy Spirit. Paul said in the new testament that he died daily. We have to crucify this old flesh. "For all that is in the world, the lust of the flesh and the lust of the eyes, and the pride of life, is not of the father, but is of the world." I John 2:16

God is Love. He does not expect us to live holy on our own accord. That is why his Son gave us a comforter when he left. "And

I will pray the Father, and he shall give you another comforter, that he may abide with you forever. I will not leave you comfortless, I will come to you." John 14:16 & 18. When Jesus said another comforter, comforter means or equals to one besides me, an addition to me, but one just like me. Jesus was telling the disciples what the comforter would do in His absence, and what He would do if He were physically present with them. All of this lets me know that God is concerned about my welfare, well-being, and well-doing. God will keep me in the palm of His hand. We do know, if you play with fire, you will get burned. "Meats for the belly, and belly for the meats, but God shall destroy both it and them. Now the body is not for fornication, but for the Lord, and the Lord for the body." 1 Corinthians 6:13

I would like to give some personal testimonies where God gave me victory and increased my faith through manifestation. I would like to start with my childhood and come up to this present time. I am sharing these testimonies to encourage your heart and let you know God has no respecter of persons. God is not slack concerning His promises. God will give you the desires of your heart in righteousness. He wants to show you that He is your husband, and He is more than enough. I got to that point in life where I did not want anybody but Him. He is real. He is a miracle worker, a burden bearer, a heavy load carrier, a rock in a weary land, a doctor in the sick room, a lawyer in the courtroom, a bridge over troubled water, a friend for the lonely, a mother for the motherless, a father for the fatherless, a brother, a sister, a teacher, a friend for the friendless, joy in sorrow, hope for tomorrow, peace in confusion, our great intercessor, our advocate, but most of all, "Our Savior."

As I shared earlier, I came up in humble beginnings, which led to great things later in life. During my 1st through 5th grade years, I did not want to let go of my mother's hand, and neither did she. Our feelings were mutual. I did not attend kindergarten; I went straight to 1st grade. Back then, kindergarten was not a requirement. I cried many mornings because I was not comfortable being away from my mom. I was so horrified to have been sent to school without knowing anyone and in a classroom with other little boys and girls that I had never seen in my life. My mother did not prepare me for that day. She never told me that I would soon have lots of new friends my age, and we would learn together, eat lunch together, and play outside together every day. I was just thrust into a big building where everyone was a stranger and different from my familiar surroundings. Nevertheless, I got over that hurdle within a month or so.

It had become a way of life for me and all the other school kids. Students were getting school day pictures made, going to the circus, or going to the library downtown on the weekend. I noticed how kids had money to buy hot lunches, milk, and cookies. They even had money to stop by the store after school in the evening time. Believe it or not, none of that fazed me. Back then, no one looked down on you or bullied you for not having. My young mind was comfortable because I felt my parents were great and they knew what was best for me. I never felt insecure, inferior, poor, or without. This went on from the 1st grade to the 4th grade.

I remember in my 5th grade year of school, we had "May Day." That was a big day; There were no classes all day, children had on new spring clothes, new shoes, new hairdos, and extra money to buy from the vending machines and there were lots of games to play. That is the year my eyes came open. I did not have new clothes or shoes, and my hair was not fixed differently. However, I did get a little extra money. My mother gave me a quarter and told me to make it last. I was so happy to get that quarter. Ever now and then, I would get three cents for a carton of milk and maybe five cents for five oatmeal cookies once a month. However, the Lord would always bless. A quarter back then was like ten dollars to me. When I got to school, kids were buying pronto pups, hot dogs, hamburgers, cotton candy, corn dogs, soda pops, ice cream, oatmeal cookies, chips, and candy. I knew I had only a quarter, which was a whole lot to me, but it was not enough to buy more than two or three items. So, I waited before I spent my quarter. Even though I was very young, I knew it was better to eat on the back end than spend my quarter in the beginning and not have anything for later. While kids were eating all day long, I just acted like I did not know what I wanted. I knew I did not have any extra money to play any games. So I ran around the yard, chased, and played. Some of my friends would let me take a bite of their food. God still kept my young heart encouraged. When I realized how much money the other students had, it was unbelievable. To me, their parents were rich or well to do. My present condition was no indication of my future potential in God. Where I started and how I ended in life was up to me.

Even though I was not as fortunate as others, I never felt poor, less fortunate, or without. I never felt like asking my parents why I could not get school day pictures, go on field trips, go to the sock hops, or why I could not buy milk and cookies every day for eight cents because I never heard my older siblings ask why. Therefore, it was just the norm and a way of life for me. My mother always taught us there will be people who will have more than you, and there will be people who will have less than you. Regardless of what you have and what you don't have, you will always be in the middle; which is alright if you read that statement with scrutiny.

That was the year our house caught on fire. We were living in my grandmother's home: me, my parents and my five siblings. Eventually, my father put us in our own home. My grandmother taught my mother and father how to live holy, how to pray, and how to discipline and raise us. We were taught how to speak up and speak out, and we were taught to look a person in the eyes when speaking to them. We could not flush the toilet every time we visited the bathroom, and we could not stand around grown people and listen to their conversations. I resented having three parents as a young child.

My grandmother was a very strict disciplinarian. She would sit between the bedroom and the kitchen. She had her readers on and down on her face, which was scary to me as a child because no one ever told me that those were readers and that was the proper way to wear them. She had a Bible and a tall switch, which stood about five feet tall in the corner. That switch was a reminder, plus she told us, "I will set you like on fire," and those words rang through our minds and little ears. We were never loud, rambunctious, disrespectful, or unruly. We were very sheltered for the most part. I can truly say, my grandmother gave us all a push in life and a push for life, including my dad, my mother, and all my siblings. She was definitely our true foundation in religion and everyday practical living. She taught my dad as if he were her son. He had an ear to hear, to obey, and follow, more than her three biological sons.

I remember my father was looking for a job and my grandmother told him to go to the prayer meetings. My father said he did not have time to go to prayer meetings, so God gave him time. He was outside mowing the lawn and something got stuck in the lawnmower. He thought the lawnmower was cut off and he put his hand underneath it, and the blade cut two of his fingers off as if they were grass. Therefore, he could not do anything with his hand for a while. So he applied for two or three jobs and waited for them to call. While he was waiting, he started attending the prayer meetings with my mother, and they carried me and my younger brother with them. The places where he put in applications called him around the same time, and my father had to make a huge decision because both companies were reputable. By him attending the prayer meetings, God led him to make the right decision. He chose the company that God gave him. My brother, my cousin, and two more of my brother's friends were also hired. My dad, brother, and my cousin worked there until they retired. My dad got very light duty with his regular pay until he retired. He had also become a pastor during that time. My brother received special privileges because he had a degree and was a pastor. He could leave for funerals and special church services and still remain on the clock. My brother and I, who attended prayer meetings, worked for the same company while we were in college.

When your parents come up in prayer meetings, in the church, and bring their children up the same way, it makes all the difference in the world. It gives them a true foundation, a love for God, increased faith, and it keeps them from a million failures. To God be the Glory for the things He has done.

At one of the schools I taught in, most of the children were raised by one parent, and the parent was young. Some of the high school girls were mothers already, so I was shocked, but it was not time to mull over spilled milk. Time was of the essence. I started teaching there at the beginning of the second semester. I told God I needed Him and needed Him right away. He told me not to eat lunch, stay in my room, cut the lights off and get in the corner and get down on my knees and pray. Well, that sounded farfetched and so out of the ordinary. That did not seem convenient for me. Praying on my knees, on the job, in the classroom, during my lunch period? Surely God could have given me another directive. God knew how to turn the flame up in those children until I could not wait to get down on my knees and pray. My beloved readers, I want you to know that when I started praying, I saw an immediate response. I saw an immediate turnaround in my students. God worked for me so quickly. My students were just like puppets and robots, and they did not know what caused the change. They knew they could not act out, talk out, or be disrespectful. When I got down on my knees in a corner of the classroom, God gave me victory over those giants' heads. With God, I was able to run through troops and leap over walls. My stamina had begun to ascend. Teachers would praise me, the three principals thought I was phenomenal, all because of the Power of Prayer. I knew from that point on that God had given me my teaching license. They made me a math chairman, put me over the school programs, put me over the majorettes, and made me a teacher cheerleader. I was the most popular teacher in the building. God had given me and my family so much favor at that school. We would get our hair done in cosmetology, clothes cleaned for a dollar, shoes repaired, food catered, and fried catfish every Friday. The Power of Prayer touches hearts, and shows favor. God said in Luke 6:38, "Give and it shall be given unto you, good measure, pressed down and shaken together and running over, shall men give into your bosom."

I thank God I obeyed, even though I was reluctant. I saw immediate action, miracles, and God turning things around for me and working on my behalf. "And all things whatsoever ye shall ask in prayer, believing, ye shall receive." Matthew 21:22 "Pray without ceasing." I Thessalonian 5:17 God is saying to keep the prayer wheel turning. When I look back, I realize, it was not about the students acting out, but it was about me. It was a certain place that God wanted me to get in Him. He was also drawing me closer to Him, increasing my faith, and teaching me the power of prayer and fasting. "Howbeit this kind goeth not out but by prayer and fasting." Matthew 17:21 "For my love they are my adversaries, but I give myself unto prayer." Psalm 109:4 I have used that prayer tool during my whole 35 years of my career. I could leave my classroom and take care of personal business. I was able to leave someone in charge, and everyone would respect that person. Students would not talk out without permission. They would not get up to sharpen their pencils without permission. They would not ask to go to the restroom or locker for any reason. When a teacher or an administrator would come and get my attention, they were as quiet as a church mouse. God could have made those students like that on day one. Again, it was something the Lord wanted to teach and show me for a testimony. I have given this testimony about the power of prayer, and many have caught on with the tests, trials, and tribulations they have faced in their lives.

I gave these students, teachers, faculty, staff, parents, and the community "love and hope" in action and deed. I asked my principal could I sponsor a trip to Mexico during Spring Break. He was always my biggest cheerleader and supporter because I changed the atmosphere of that school and was able to teach and discipline those students in my classroom. It was nothing too small or great that I could not ask for. For the trip to Mexico, he told me if I could pull it off, I could carry the students. I took them to Mexico, and that blew their minds and the community. Some of those students, if not most, had not been any further than downtown and South Memphis. They were ecstatic. As a new teacher, that was a big task. Ms. Judy Smith, a Spanish teacher at Wesley High, went with me and carried a few of her students from her class. She succored me every step of the way. I met this man, who had the approval of the board, Curtis Green. We used his bus company to make the trip. Little did I know, he would help me throughout my career in carrying students across the country. Other colleagues, Judy Smith, Tonya Haley, Gloria Watsons, Lorene Malone, and Keith Watsons, and others, would use his company and buses. We had the time of our lives and untold memories. The faculty and principal would come to me for any kind of program presentations, welcoming board members, and extra-curricular activities and festivities.

My principal, Mitch Walker, had a few health issues. As he was coming back to Memphis from a tournament in Nashville, he pulled over on the side of the road, had a heart attack, and died at the age of 52. We had just honored him for giving back to the community at the Black History Program. He was a graduate of that school. I spoke at his wake and funeral for the community, our school, and the board of education. It was an easy task because I had all of his information, life accolades, awards, and career already prepared from honoring him a few weeks earlier. The school and community were bemused and baffled that a man who had shown so much love to the community, his job, school, faculty, and staff was gone for good. It was so untimely. He was the kind of principal that would tell the cafeteria staff to let the students eat all they wanted until the food was gone because it was the only meal some students would have. He would empathetically tell the teachers to do everything they could to help the students graduate because this would be the only success some would experience. Some of those students were the first ones to graduate in their families, and that will be as far as they'd go. He used his own money to help students with their personal needs. He was born to be a principal over poverty-stricken students. Regardless of all the good you do, someone is going to complain. Some would say he was doing too much or he was giving too much, or that he was just handicapping the students. Some would even say, if they were him, they would have done it this way or that way. The Bible says, "It is an honour for a man to cease from strife, but every fool will be meddling." Proverbs 20:3

We would normally have faculty meetings on Wednesdays after school. One time, he called an emergency meeting that was not on a Wednesday. Everyone wanted to know what was going on and what the meeting all about. When we got to the meeting, he promised us that he would not hold us long. He said, "I know I have not met your expectations or done things the way you would've liked me to. All I am going to say is, when the Board of Education selected me, 'They Knew You.' You all are dismissed." The teachers were shocked because he had always been easy-going and nonchalant, but when he addressed something, he addressed it.

I remember another situation with him that I will never forget. A student was suspended and the child was very irate and disrespectful toward the mother. You could see that the student was the one running his household. When the mother said something to her son, the boy responded, "You talk like a fool." The principal said the son was not the problem. He said the mother was the problem for not raising him properly. So we asked him how did the mother look, and how did she respond? He said she looked just like a child and took him back home. The principal said the student should have gone home and kicked his mother under the bed. We laughed, screamed, and hollered. This was back in the 80s when times were much better and parents had control over their children. Children are raising their parents now. I loved that principal, school, students, and faculty. It was not like that at first. The students were hard-headed and challenging. I was just a few years older than they were and had just graduated from college. God strategically sent me to that particular school so I could be stretched and tested. I had no choice but to get closer to God and learn of Him. I did, and it worked. Whatever the problem is, whatever you might be facing, or whatever struggles you might be going through, they all come to point you to Jesus. Get to know Him and the Father. Above all, you need the Holy Ghost, which is the keeping power.

He will keep you during your hours of temptation. "Mine eyes are ever toward the Lord, for He shall pluck my feet out of the net." Psalm 25:15 That was one of the schools where I would spend my lunch break on my knees praying. I'd turn the light off, get in a corner, and pray as the Lord instructed me to. I saw immediate results. The more I prayed, the more the Lord worked for me.

I taught over there one more year and transferred to Hills Jr. High. That was the biggest junior high school in the state of Tennessee. The Board had given me three schools to choose from, and I asked the Lord for direction. I had just received the Baptism of the Holy Ghost, with the evidence of speaking in tongue. God led me to Acts 1:8, "But ye shall receive power, after that the Holy Ghost is come upon you; and ye shall be witnesses unto me both in Jerusalem, and in all Judaea, and in Samaria, and unto the uttermost part of the earth." God magnified "uttermost part of the earth" to me and uttermost means farthest in this case. I lived in South Memphis with my parents at the time, and Hills Jr. High was the farthest because it was in North Memphis. So there I went. Hills Jr. High was the school for me. Not knowing my husband would find me there, shortly. I will get back to that later. When I was teaching at Hills Jr. High, I met David T. Jones. He was a very nice, prosperous young man and very family-oriented. He had everything going for him physically and financially. I really liked him and my parents did as well. I knew I could not have a boyfriend or date at this point. I was a baby saint, adjusting to living wholeheartedly for the Lord, and focusing on my career and students, and going back to get my Master's Degree. I had no room for temptation, so I let him go. My parents were praying to that effort as well. I had a lot going on, so I had to be totally committed to God and my new lifestyle of holiness. My parents told me it was either holiness or nothing. You cannot have God and shake hands with the devil. So, I chose God over David T. Jones. What a letdown, but it paid off in the end. You cannot beat "God's giving" no matter how hard you try. I gave God my life, my soul, my talents, my time, and my tithes. I went to the extreme top as a math teacher. God blessed me more than I could ever ask or think.

I was always selected to go out of town for math seminars, and come back and show other teachers what I learned. All my expenses were paid, and extra money was given to me at my own disposal. I was selected Teacher of the Month and Teacher of the Year. I was nominated "Most Favorite Teacher." Students would try to dress like me, talk like me, and mimic me in most of the schools I taught in. I was able to take off seven school days with pay to attend the "Holy Convocation Conference," take my own personal vacation during the school time with pay, and meet all of my doctors' appointments without taking off from work. Teachers would keep my students with the principal's approval. I would determine the activities for the teachers at Christmas time, plan the party, and choose the venue. I would choose the activities for the senior class throughout the year. I was overseer over the main events. God would give me so much favor and leverage. I had more power than the assistant principals. I knew how to carry myself and respect them as well, so I would not create any enemies. For the most part, I had the support of the principal, his staff, parents, and the community. I can truly say I had limitless favor. I knew God did it and designed it because I exemplified Him in the classroom daily.

Whatever the students asked me, I would give them a scriptural answer based on God's Word. It was not an outside show. It was because I was raised that way. The Word was embedded in me for life, not knowing one day I would become a minister and later an ordained elder. God gave me extraordinary favor because of my early morning prayer life. God would prove himself strong, over and over again. Whatever I would put my hands to, it would prosper at an early age. I knew the key to a perfect life, and that was to have an early morning prayer life. I would give God an hour a day before I went to work. Prayer changes and conditions things. My prayer life is my permanent lifestyle.

During this, I was introduced to my husband through a teacher. She liked him but did not like the church denomination he was in because they believed in speaking in tongues. She was totally against that, so she wanted me to meet him. She felt he would be good for me. I told her, if you do not want him, I do not want him either.

The three of us went to the Orpheum to see the play, *Mama, I Want to Sing*. Tonya, the teacher, left to go to the restroom, and he started up a conversation with me, showing he had an interest in me. Again, I was not interested but flattered. The three of us would go on dates. That was perfect for me. I was focusing on my Master's Degree. I did not want to be in a relationship, but I did like going to dinner with them. Later, he called and asked if he and I could go out together. I said okay because he was a gentleman, generous, respectful, and extremely kind to me, my family, and my friends. He would pick me up and take me to dinner every Saturday, any restaurant of my choice. Then, he started getting involved in my school work. He was a profound reader, and he started writing all of my papers for me. I was so impressed. He started sending flowers to my home and on the job. He did all the nice things that were eye-catching and would get the attention of every onlooker. Eventually, we started dating. He respected me. He never asked me to be intimate with him. That went a long way with me. I went on and received my degree. His mother exclaimed that his name should have been on there and not mine. I went the following year and worked on my third degree, which is called a plus 45 degree.

Graduating with my Master's Degree in the midst of teaching.

I had this friend named Chandra Hines, who was a teacher also. We received all our degrees together. It is good to befriend someone in school who has the same interest as you. We were very inspirational and motivational to each other. We had each other's back. I thank God for her today. We both received our three degrees together from the same school. Afterward, I got engaged to Richard Terry in November of 1987 during our Holy Convocation in Memphis, Tennessee. He picked out a very nice, good clarity diamond from Bailey, Banks, and Biddle, a top diamond store in Memphis.

The diamond was top quality, but it was too small. I wanted something big and eye-catching, so I cut straight to the chase and told him and he honored my request. He bought me a beautiful solitaire and two wedding bands with baguettes. He was the ideal man or prince. We started making plans for our wedding because we chose to get married in five months. We both knew you do not know a person until you live with them. Also, long dating leads to temptations. So, we had a beautiful rainbow wedding with all kinds of doctors, teachers, attorneys, preachers, and the like in attendance. I think we had about 20 people in our wedding. What a fairy tale! When I was in the eighth grade, my sister had a rainbow wedding, and it was so magical and stunning. I didn't know I would have the same kind of wedding two decades later. It is good when your siblings are positive role models. I also attended the same college as my sisters. I became a teacher like my elder sister and had a rainbow wedding like she did. She was the reason I am saved today.

Chapter 4

Journeying with God in Control

I remember after graduation, my sister called and asked our mom, "Has Aretha gotten saved yet?" My mom said, "No." That really pierced my heart. It was like a judgement day message. The Lord magnified that in my heart and spirit. I was convicted, and my heart was pricked. It was like God was speaking, and that statement rested on me. I felt like that was my final chance. I had just lost my best friend's sister two years before that. She was only 19 and was about to turn 20 a few weeks later. She was in a terrible car accident with her husband, brother, and his wife. She did not have one scratch on her, but her neck was broken. God will call you at any time and any age. She had one little daughter, about one or two years old. All of that was running through my mind. "For unto whomsoever much is given, of him shall be much required." Luke 12:48b It means we are responsible for what we have. If we have been blessed with talents, wealth, knowledge, and time, it is expected that we benefit others, and above all, live for God wholeheartedly. You must have a day-to-day relationship with Him, as you would with your significant other. God is not and will not compete with anyone because He is a jealous God. "For the Lord thy God is a jealous God among you, Lest the anger of the Lord thy God be kindled against thee, and destroy thee front off the face of the earth." Deuteronomy 6:15 "For thou shalt worship no other god: for the LORD, whose name is Jealous, is a jealous God" Exodus 34:14

I answered the call, not many days hence. I was the youngest girl in the family, but she called my name. Nevertheless, I answered the call when I accepted Christ as my personal savior and started walking with Him. My sister, who was four years older than me, accepted Christ as well. It was the first week of January 1979. I could hardly wait to go to church and openly accept the invitation. Paul said this thing was not done in a corner.

Well, that seventh day of January 1979, there was a big snowstorm. No one was going out, but I still kept the promise that I made. I went into the restroom and prepared for the day. I started talking to the Lord. I had opened my heart and mind to Him. I asked Him to forgive me of my sins, and I wanted to be saved. God heard me and He came into my life that day. He saved me and adopted me into the royal family. He told me I was His. That morning, I was connected. A change came over me right there in the bathroom. It was an experience like no other. God definitely changed me without the aid of a pastor. I had a made-up mind and God knew I was sincere. I thank God that I did not let Satan trick me into putting it off until the following Sunday. I might not have had the same mindset. I could have died without having Christ in my life or as my personal savior. I did not tell my mother or anyone. I just started going to the daytime prayer meetings. One of the mothers openly asked me if I was saved, and my mother looked at me and I said, "Yes, ma'am." My mother looked at me and said, "She is lying in the church." She looked at me again, and God showed her the change. She did not know that I had gotten converted in the bathroom while taking a bath. Then, I began to tell everybody. I told my family, my best friend, and my boyfriend. My best friend and my boyfriend knew that when I am in something, I am in it all the way. They told me that they hated that I had changed because they knew my lifestyle was not going to be the same, and we would no longer be interested in the same things. I gradually severed ties with them.

In college, I was very popular. God had blessed me with a very nice smile. I wore beautiful and fashionable clothes because my uncle had gotten me a job at the Bulk Mail Center, a subsidiary of the United States Postal Service. I worked the 5 pm - 2 am shift and helped two of my friends get jobs through my uncle. We made "big money". We bought any and everything we could think of. This was long money for a sophomore in college. The money I was making was the take-home pay for a man, his wife, and five children. We would shop at exclusive boutiques, only where the upper crust shopped, Helen of Memphis, Snooty Fox, Gerber's Department Store, and M.M. Cohn. I mostly wore dresses and skirts because of my upbringing. Oh, how my wardrobe took over the campus, mainly because my clothes were exclusive, conservative, yet fashionable dresses for rich girls. My morale and self-esteem were over the top. I never was arrogant. I just kept my genuine, God-given smile. I even had the nerve to get blonde in my hair and a makeover on my teeth. I was ready for Miss America. I can hear my dad saying now, "Child get somewhere and sit down."

I pledged Delta Sigma Theta Sorority. I had many sorority and fraternity brothers, Omega Psi Phi. I ran for Miss Whisper University and became an Omega Pearl. I performed in several Greek Shows. All the carnal things I did were basic clean fun. God gave me favor with my professors, even though I was not living for Him. "Thou shalt keep therefore his statutes, and his commandments, which I command thee this day that it may go well with thee, and with thy children after thee, and that thou mayest prolong thy days upon the earth, which the Lord thy God giveth thee, for ever. Deuteronomy 4:40

I was selected to be on the opening page of our senior yearbook for being nominated Miss Senior. I was standing by a Rolls Royce and a Show dog. I thought that was so cool. I had no idea it was indicative of my future. The school staff picked that scene for me. At that time, I did not think anything of it. I was only 21. I did not know then that God was in that. The staff probably saw something in me that I could not see. Mostly all of my professors liked me, males and females. God gave me a winsome personality. Everybody knew I was a Christian by my dress, mannerism, and the girls I associated with. I got a chance to taste a little of the world, which I thought had so much to offer me. It was okay, same ol', same ol'. My parents instilled sanctification, holiness, and righteousness in me so, the little time I stuck my foot out there, it wasn't all that my friends said it was. However, I did have some good times, fun times, and cool times. It was always on my mind. Choose ye this day whom you will serve. What if God calls you home and you do not have a personal relationship with Him? I could always hear my mom say, "The children of Israel cannot do what the world does, because you know right from wrong. You were bought with a price. What if God calls you home and you have no relationship with Him. A disobedient child does not live his days out." I did experience going to the games, dances, Greek shows, out-of-town games, happy hours, one or two clubs, and it was BORING. I enjoyed going to see the Isley Brothers, Commodores, and Stevie Wonder. I tasted the world! I had a choice to make. Choose ye this day whom ye will serve. Will it be God and His son, Jesus, who saved me from my sins, sanctified me, filled me with the Holy Ghost with the evidence of speaking in tongues?

I breathed and lived the worldly culture because Satan had control of my life. I did what I wanted to do without the worries of God watching me. Now, there was a complete change in my life, and I had to learn the culture of the kingdom. I can tell you right now, you do not learn the culture in one day, one week, one month, or even a year. It is a beautiful life experience. The more you grow, the more you know. Living Holy is a business, and seeking God is a lifestyle. Like a baby, I kept standing up, walking, stumbling, and falling, but the Lord was right there to take the training wheels off my ride with Him. Every time I stumbled or fell, the Lord was right there to pick me up with no condemnation. "For God sent not His son into the world to condemn the world, but that the world through Him might be saved." John 3:17

God's love is real, and it is truly genuine. Once you walk with God wholeheartedly, you will have happiness, peace, victory, and love like never before. You will feel and experience all kinds of voids in your life if you don't. Once you taste that "Love Divine" and walk away, God will never walk away from you because He said He is married to you. "Turn, O backsliding children, saith the Lord; for I am married unto you." Jeremiah 3:14a If there ever be a separation or divorce from God, you did it. Every day you breathe, His arms are stretched out for you "to come." "Today if ye will hear his voice, harden not your hearts, as in the provocation." Hebrews 3:15 "Now the just shall live by faith, but if any man draw back, my soul shall have no pleasure in him." Hebrew 10:38

When you have a day-to-day personal relationship or a daily secret closet relationship with God, God will adopt you into His royal family, and you will become a joint heir of God, and joint-heirs with Christ. We already know, if you are part of the royal family, you have everything at your "Beck and Call" which is to be entirely subservient to them. There are many blessings and benefits in walking with God. Anyone who does not walk with God is living beneath their privileges. The song 'What A Friend We Have in Jesus' tells us to carry everything to God in prayer. Have we trials and temptations? Is there trouble anywhere? We should never be discouraged. Take it to the Lord in prayer. "Ask, and it shall be given you; seek, and ye shall find; knock, and it shall be opened unto you: For every one that asketh receiveth; and he that seeketh findeth; and to him that knocketh it shall be opened." Matthew 7:7-8 "If you be willing and obedient, you shall eat the good of the land." Isaiah 1:19

Chapter 5

Knowing God is a Lifetime Experience

I can truly say that Jesus is the Best Thing that ever happened to me. Jesus is not just a thing, whereas you attend church to praise Him and worship Him, hear a good Word, the choir sings melodiously, and you dance and cry. You notice how pretty the people are dressed in their Sunday best. When you have a relationship with God, He addresses the whole man, from the crown of your head to the sole of your feet. God blesses you in every aspect of your life. What concerns you also concerns God. He abides in you. "Jesus answered and said unto him, If a man love me, he will keep my Words, and my Father will love him, and we will come unto him, and make our abode with him." John 14:23 As long as God abides on the inside, He will help you naturally, physically, financially, and spiritually. Things will always go better with God. Even though the Hebrew boys were in the fiery furnace, it made all the difference in the world, when the "Fourth One" got in the fire with them. "Then Nebuchadnezzar the king was astonished, and rose up in haste, and spake, and said unto his counsellors, Did not we cast three men bound into the midst of the fire? They answered and said unto the king, True, O king. He answered and said, Lo, I see four men loose, walking in the midst of the fire, and they have no hurt; and the form of the fourth is like the Son of God." Daniel 3:24-25 God will not abide in an unclean temple. "What? Know ye not that your body is the temple of the Holy Ghost which is in you, which ye have of God, and ye are not your own? For ye are bought with a price: therefore glorify God in your body, and in your spirit, which are God's." 1 Corinthians 6:19-20

Every day of your life, God walks with you, and He talks to you through His Word. You must pick up your Bible every day and read it. He will guide you. Just open the Bible and read wherever you have turned to in the Bible, and He will have a message. If you do not get your answer or something you have been pondering about the first time you open the Bible, close it and reopen it. You will be surprised; your answer will be right there. God wants you to read His Word because the Word is Him. He wants the Bible to be your number one book, your novel, your love book, your mystery book, your action book, and above all, your romance book because God is Love. "In the beginning was the Word and the Word was with God, and the Word was God. The same was in the beginning with God." John 1:1-2 I learned that when you have a personal relationship with God, He is going to breathe on you to fast twice a week. "I fast twice a week." Luke 18:12a "Moreover when ye fast, be not, as the hypocrites, of a sad countenance: for they disfigure their faces, that they may appear unto men to fast. Verily I say unto you, They have their reward." Matthew 6:16 A personal relationship with God leads you to get up early and pray before you leave for school, work, or church, or before starting your day. "I love them that love me, and they that seek me early shall find me." Proverbs 8:11

You want to seek God early, before the phone rings or before turning on the TV or radio. God wants first place in your life. He sets precedence over all things; family, friends, work, and hobbies. Some people get up jogging, walking, or exercising. He wants to be first place, so He can reward you and know that you love Him with all your heart and soul. "For he that cometh to God must believe that he is and that he is a rewarder of them that diligently seek him." Hebrews 11:6 Praying is a sincere desire of the heart. "Call unto me, and I will answer and shew thee great and mighty things, which thy knowest not." Jeremiah 33:3 Anyone you have a relationship with, you want to be able to communicate with them when you get ready. God is always waiting, looking, listening, and watching to hear from you daily. So please let Him in. You want to go to church and fellowship with the saints. "Not forsaking the assembling of ourselves together, as the manner of some is; but exhorting one another: and so much the more, as ye see the day approaching." Hebrews 10:25 We want to encourage and warn each other that judgement day is drawing near. Every time one dies, he or she has had their judgement day. "And as it is appointed unto men once to die, but after this the judgement." Hebrews 9:27

I found that being a member of a church and being totally involved is important and helps in a profitable lifestyle. First of all, you have great fellowship, and the church members become your family. They celebrate you and the things that are meaningful to you. You have someone to share your feelings, thoughts, etc. I found one of my best friends by attending a summer prayer meeting when I was off from teaching in the summer. We have been friends for over 30 years. God put us together. Just on the surface, we would not have chosen each other as best friends, but God did. God never makes a mistake. God knows what is best for each of us. He is foresighted. He knows who we need down the road through sicknesses, losses, financial woes, and spiritual growth. He knows we need someone we can share personal things with and someone who will tell the truth whether we like it or not. "A man that hath friends must shew himself friendly: and there is a friend that sticketh closer than a brother." Proverbs 18:24

I went to a small church, and that church was basically involved in everyone's life. We supported each other during Valentine's Day, Mother's Day, Father's Day, Easter, Birthdays, Thanksgiving, Christmas, and New Year's Eve. You have support throughout the entire year. You never feel lonely unless you have isolated yourself. You also want to be actively involved in a church home, in case you get married, start a family, purchase a new home or apartment. That leads to bridal showers, bachelor parties, weddings, baby showers, house blessings, and housewarming parties, etc. You will have the support of your church family. Everybody wants to be celebrated.

Jesus had many disciples and followers. His friends were Lazarus, Mary, Martha, and John, his cousin and the most beloved disciple. "Therefore his sisters sent unto him, saying, Lord, behold, he whom thou lovest is sick." John 11:3 "Now Jesus loved Martha, and her sister, and Lazarus." John 11:5 "Now there was leaning on Jesus' bosom one of his disciples, whom Jesus loved." John 13:23

Your friends and family in the church will always pray with you, pray for you, keep you lifted in prayer, even when they may not know what is going on in your life. Jesus will intercede through them on your behalf. Going to church on Sundays always made my week better and I was able to endure my tests and trials. God would always carry me through because I would have given Him quality time by attending church services. Your pastor will expound on the Word until it becomes part of your everyday conversation. Going to church was more than just a tradition or a duty. You are around people who profess the same spiritual views as you, present themselves as a living sacrifice, are totally sold out to God, and make Him first place in their lives.

I also enjoyed the testimonies of the people and their victories that were won. The testimonies were very encouraging and uplifting. If God did it for them, He will do it for me. God has no respecter of person. Testimonies always gave me hope. Going to church for us was like going to the hospital. Everybody goes to the hospital for a different ailment, sickness, disease, or other causes. Whatever the issue is, everyone is looking and depending on the nurse and doctors' expertise or field to address their problem, get them well, give them a solution along with meals, and send them home feeling better. Some may even die at the hospital without ever going back home. Whatever their lot or fate, they went to the hospital, some emergency room, some intensive care, and some went to the morgue. What am I saying? The same way people trust going to the doctor and going to the hospital, we should trust even more going to the church. They told me the church is the saint's hospital. "If you can have it, God can heal it." God is the doctor in the sick room. God knows all about us because He is the one that made us in His own image. God is a heart fixer and a mind regulator. God is the only one that can give you a new heart, lungs, or brain, without having a transplant. A person can have the same disease or diagnosis that you have, and they may be in terrible pain; some have even died. Your faith brought you through, and you have peace because you know God is going to heal you. And until He does, He said in His Word, "To appoint unto them that mourn in Zion, to give unto them beauty for ashes, the oil of joy for mourning, the garment of praise for the spirit of heaviness; that they might be called trees of righteousness, the planting of the LORD, that he might be glorified." Isaiah 61:3

I also found there are many ways to be active in the church. You can sing in the choir, serve as an usher, work with the children's ministry, teach a Sunday School class, work with the outreach ministry, work as office staff, serve on the hospitality committee, drive for the pastor and his wife, clean up the church, be a cook for the church, etc. There is always something a person can do in the body of Christ because only what you do for Christ will last. "Therefore, my beloved brethren be ye steadfast, unmoveable, always abounding in the work of the Lord, forasmuch as ye know that your labour is not in vain in the Lord." 1 Corinthians 15:58 Our conduct or our actions should be influenced by knowing and understanding that we will have to give an account to Christ as Judge for every thought, word, or deed. "Wherefore we labour that whether present or absent, we may be accepted of him. For we must all appear before the judgement seat of Christ that every one may receive the things done in his body, according to that he hath done, whether it be good or bad." 2 Corinthians 5:9-10 The poet C.T. Studd said it best in layman's term. *"Only one life, twill soon be past, only what's done for Christ will last."* "But he that doeth the will of God abideth for ever." 1 John 2:17b It is good to excel in working for God and know that the hard work we do for the Lord is not in vain.

When I became a Christian, living for God was a choice. It was a new life and very unfamiliar to me, but I knew deep in my heart, I was on the right road for life. Did I miss my old friends and boyfriend? Yes, Yes, and Yes, and God knew I did, but I chose "CHOICE" (Choosing Higher Other Interests over Choice Entanglements). God knew I had a made-up mind to follow Him, so God moved my boyfriend off the street from where I lived, because that was a great temptation being a baby saint and not having the Holy Ghost. My best friend got married and had twins. That was another relief. My family loved my best friend and boyfriend a whole lot. I knew they were not part of my destiny. I had already been a high school teacher for two months, so that was a great distraction in my life at the age of 22. So, memories of my best friend and boyfriend began to fade away.

The Holy Ghost is your keeping power. I did not receive the Holy Ghost with the evidence of speaking in tongues when I got converted, as some did and even do today. I received the Holy Ghost a few years later with the evidence of speaking in tongues. My interest was totally on my career, teaching a very rigid subject, math, dealing with teenage attitudes, girlfriend and boyfriend drama, learning how to be a strict disciplinarian at the age of 22, and at the same time, being a nice teacher, so I had to learn balance at a young age, where the students were only five years younger than me. But God was with me every step of the way.

My first school was Wesley High. God strategically placed me next door to a teacher who was eight years older than me, and she was a new convert. She was an asset to my career and also my spiritual walk with the Lord. I was 22 years old, and she was 30. She was single like me. She had been teaching eight years before I started. She was able to help me in so many facets. It paid off tremendously. She taught me the ins and outs. I would call her no matter what school I was teaching at, and she would give me insight on a lot of things. She taught me how to do out-of-town trips with my students, and she traveled with me when I took my first trip with my students to Mexico. She was a Spanish teacher. She was an asset to me and my students.

She and I continued to stay connected throughout our careers. Sometimes, we would go years without hearing or seeing each other, but when we did get together, we made up for lost times. We would spend seven to eight hours on the phone catching up. Sometimes, she would come to visit me or I would go visit her. We would do lunch together and just enjoy each other's company. We did this until the end of my career.

She helped to decorate my huge condo on the river. She even visited my new home and helped in arranging the furniture she helped me to pick out. I'm about to talk about that miracle in a moment. She came every day except Saturday or Sunday like clockwork. She had an interest in my home as if it was hers. She was definitely God-sent naturally, spiritually, and financially. She passed away in April of 2018 from cancer. I had just come back from visiting my sister for a month in Flint, Michigan.

I had become an ordained Elder and had three speaking engagements. The Lord allowed me to get off the plane and see her before she took her last breath. A friend went along with me to Baptist Desoto Hospital in Mississippi. We prayed over her, and she died a few hours later. I appreciate my brother calling and telling me things were not looking good for her. God put an urgency in me to go and see her. I asked her family permission if I could dress her for her home-going celebration. They were glad for the relief during their time of sorrow and told me it was an honor to them for me to take on that responsibility. I ordered her a white suit from Lily and Taylor in New York. I had pearls on her neck and pearls on her wrist. I had a beautiful wig that made her look so young and beautiful. Ironically, her favorite niece, who she was instrumental in raising, had bought the same exact wig in Texas. So, we used the wig her niece purchased. She and I were both happy, and we were glad how everything came together for my close friend. I will never forget her. She was instrumental in my travels abroad doing missionary work. She did missionary work in 30 countries. God really blessed her home-going celebration. She was not an outgoing person and very reserved. God gave her a funeral like a big celebrity. God said in his Word, "Behold, I will be with you always, even unto the end of the world." She had a Holy Ghost-filled, hand-clapping, tongue-speaking, foot-stomping Homegoing Celebration, as quiet and reserved as she was. God gave her what she was all about, building churches and schools in 30 countries. He did not forget her labor of love. Hebrew 6:10, "For God is not unrighteous to forget your work and labor of love, which we have shewed toward his name, in that ye, have ministered to the saints, and do minister." God remembers when others forget. We only taught in the same school for one year, but we became lifelong colleagues and friends. I thank God for her today. I thank God for her being concerned about me during the infancy of my career and my new walk with Him. I will never forget it. Here I am 40 years later, still holding up the blood-stained banner and walking with God.

I left Western Hills School and went to Hays Jr. High School. I taught math, and I taught the Bible. I was young; I was just a novice. The students would ask me about my life and why I was different from the other teachers. I would tell them I had a relationship with God and that I was saved now. Not the kind of saved they called saved. I told them I did more than confess with my mouth and shook the preacher's hand. I told them my whole lifestyle had changed. My walk, talk, and conduct, as well as my friends, had changed. I made a 180-degree change in my life that would lead straight to the Bible. That kept their little minds in wonderment. Of course, God was in it too. He wanted those kids to be exposed to righteousness as well as holiness. Most of my students were unchurched because their parents did not attend church. So the only way they would be exposed to God would be through me, Aretha Coleman. I still did not know what was being exemplified until well into my career. God had it that way so it would not seem like a task but more like a student-teacher conversation, where the students asked questions, and I was equipped to give out all the answers. God is an Awesome God. They did take prayer out of school but not under my watch. God gave me so many open doors and advantages to go forth. Man, did I go forth. "The kingdom of heaven suffereth violence, and the violent take it by force." Matthew 11:12b

God knows I took it by force, being a novice. I left there after two years and went to Everetts High and did what God had created me to do. I wrote a Christian Easter Play promoting Jesus and not the Easter bunny or eggs, and that went over well in North Memphis. God has always given me great support from the parents and communities at every school I taught in. During my first four years of teaching, I had a saved and sanctified principal. Therefore, I felt comfortable teaching God and promoting holiness. He did not know anything about it. I was a baby saint, it was my new lifestyle and language. I wasn't trying to be seen. It was just God shining through me, and the students were amazed.

I would always carry my students on a Spring Break escape trip. We would travel to Florida, Texas, and New York with side trips to Baltimore, Maryland, Washington, D.C., 1600 Pennsylvania Avenue, and Boston. But out of all the cities, I loved New York the most. I spent every Spring Break with my students going to New York. We had so much fun and favor all the way there and back. It was a 19-hour drive on the bus. We watched movies, slept, ate, and visited each other on the bus. It never seemed like 19-hours. Those were the most enjoyable bus hours of our lives. With children, you will always have excitement and fun. There was never a dull moment. I remember stopping at a Marshall's store in the city for a pit stop. One of my students told everyone to go in there and buy one thing they wanted. I was so green. That was another story, but we will talk about it later. He paid for everybody's purchase. Again, we will talk about that later. I was only 27 years old, a novice, and a church girl. "We still will talk later."

I thank God for allowing me to go on trips with my students without any problems or complications. I would always have excellent bus drivers that were children-friendly and had lots of patience. We had very flexible bus drivers. Out of my 35 years of teaching, there was one bus driver I had concerns about. He knew he was a long-range bus driver, and we would make a lot of pit-stops and restaurant breaks during the 19-hour trip. It seems as if everything was very frustrating to him. He was impatient, not friendly, and mostly on edge. I do not know whether he was tired, sleepy, or afraid of the road. He was very questionable. Nevertheless, he did not alter the atmosphere or the happiness of our trip.

I did not have children of my own. Therefore, the students at school became my family. The good times, traveling, and exposure I would give to my own personal children, I gave it to my students with pleasure. I taught my students how to do public speaking, have good manners and etiquette, about proper eating, how to dress for the occasion, get discounts on items, how to buy the larger quantity of something and not the smaller one because it saves money. I taught them how to open bank accounts, how to establish good credit and how to have a good credit score and the purposes and usages of a nice credit score. I taught them everyday living and practical living. I taught them the appropriate time to start a family and the quickest way to get rid of your boyfriend, "is getting pregnant by him." I taught them the importance of going to college, enrolling in the service, or taking up a trade and the importance of being self-supportive and independent. I told them everyone needs salvation and education to be successful. If you can't have both, choose salvation because it will take you from earth to glory. I knew what my calling was in life, naturally and spiritually. I hit the ground running with the torch until the race was over. "I have fought a good fight, I have finished my course, I have kept the faith." 2 Timothy 4:7

I worked 35 years until the day was done. God was with me every step of the way. He gave me tenacity, stamina, and boldness. I loved my career to pieces. I would not have traded it for any other career. The students were my joy and my career was exciting and fun. When it came to an end, I was ready to walk out the door and not look back. Do I miss my career? No, but I do miss the students immensely. Children keep you young and going. They bring a lot of energy to the table and are never winding. I never had children and never missed the opportunity of being a mother because the students made me feel like I was their mother, counselor, big sister, and so much more. I never had a dull moment in my career. It is hard to have a dull moment or a boring day after teaching 150-180

Senior Class Week!

students a year. Somebody will make you laugh about anything. "A merry heart doeth good like a medicine, but a broken spirit drieth the bones." Proverbs 17:22

After leaving that particular school, I went to another school out north. The principal there was a bully. He bullied and cussed so many teachers. One teacher had a nervous breakdown because of him, and other teachers were intimidated by him. I was the new kid on the block, and I was young. I went to his office one day, without permission from his secretary and without being announced, and I told him, "Whatever you say to me better be professional because I pray." He looked at me terrified and yelled with all his might, "Get out of my office!" So many teachers were afraid, crying, and going home. I had the greater on the inside. "Ye are of God, little children, and have overcome them, because greater is he that is in you, than he that is in the world." I John 4:4. He could not do anything with me because, number one, he knew I was a saint. He knew the school board and so many big people at the Board of Education loved me. So, he thought of something to ruffle my feathers with. He announced that teachers could not eat in their classrooms during their lunch period. They either had to eat in the cafeteria or eat in the teacher's lounge. I was not fond of either one because I liked to eat alone or sometimes read the Bible or meditate. That was my personal time to myself without students or anyone. I would still eat something periodically. He would make an effort to come to my room and peek in. Not one time did he catch me. He could not do anything with me. I was an excellent teacher, a great disciplinarian, had a great rapport with my supervisor, and my students loved me. He just did not appreciate me walking into his office and making that statement. I told my math supervisor about him, and he did not understand why the principal would address me that way, being that I was a great teacher and an excellent disciplinarian. My principal told my supervisor that if anyone from the board would come to evaluate my teaching, he would take them directly to Mrs. Coleman-Terry's room. When he told me that, I was dumbfounded. My principal tried to make me think that he had beef with me, but I thank God for stepping in and revealing the truth to me. I would not say that particular principal liked me, even though he came to my wedding and said it was a class act. The bottom line was he respected my professionalism and character. As I got older, I learned that respect means more than love. I did not work every day to be loved, but I wanted to be respected. Respect means you admire someone or something deeply as a result of their abilities, qualities, or achievements. Love is a great interest and pleasure in something or a feel for a deep romantic or sexual attachment to someone. I choose the first.

I had taken off a whole week to go to Alaska with my husband, and I chose to use my sick days. The principal was furious because he knows I come to work every day and never take off unless it is for my religious convention that everyone in the city knows about. He came down to my room and asked my students if they knew why I was absent. The students told him that I went to Alaska with my husband. He wrote me up when I got back and sent me to the Board of Education. The superintendent was so nice, kind, polite, and admirable and asked me about the trip. I told her about it, and she said it was good for teachers to gain that kind of experience. She thanked me for coming in and sent a letter through me to my principal. Again, I am laughing as I write. She said in the letter to my principal, these words, and I quote, "Excuse her, and that is between her and God where she went for a week." I am sure if he could, he would have shot bullets out of his mouth. He realized at that point he could not do anything with this 30-year-old teacher. God was for me, who could be against me. End of story.

I left that school and went to another neighboring school, still on a mission for the Lord. I was over the Student Government Association. I started a club for young ladies to build their self-esteem. I wrote a play and produced it in the community during the springtime. It went over well. The title was, "*I am not waiting on the Easter bunny, I am waiting on God.*" I gave my principal a big appreciation day, with all the clubs and organizations contributing, along with members from the Board of Education. God blessed it tremendously. We had a great big dinner afterward at one of the famous restaurants with the teachers and staff, following the program after school. That was my last year there.

As a teacher, I was a blessing to my students, and I was so blessed in my husband finding me through a colleague there. I left there and went to Mallory Jr. High, the number one optional school in Memphis, where parents camped out and spent nights to ensure that their children attended that school. That was the top public junior high school that had better activities and amenities than their private, neighboring schools had in education and extracurricular activities. It was a multicultural school with multi-cultural learning, but they were taught tolerance and differences. I feel every individual needs to learn the importance of respecting one another's culture, ethnic background, and religion. The children were from neighborhoods all across the city. It was very elite. The children were college-bound and took advanced placement courses, etc. Their parents were doctors, attorneys, veterinarians, pastors, priests, principals, teachers, city officials, the mayor of the city, or in Shelby County Government. If your parents were somebody, you attended that school.

I did not have the opportunity to teach the very elite students during the eight years I was at that school. God gave me the traditional students. That means they might not have scored high on state tests, but they had high academic grades and were college-bound. Some students do not do well on timed tests. That does not mean they are not smart, but that is the way their cookie crumbles. Some students take traditional courses because they do not want to be under pressure to learn. They want to learn, enjoy life, and not be locked in a box under pressure and competing. Some students have been taught to compete all their lives, and when it is time to attend college, they flunk out. Many do not want to attend right after high school. Sometimes they are burned out on education, whereas some traditional students enjoyed both sides of the coin. They mixed a lot of leisure with their education and still obtained a scholarship or a full ride to the college of their choice, and could not wait to attend college. They weren't just education driven, they were an all-around student; nevertheless, whichever stance they chose, they still had to be focused and stay the course. Some students put their eyes on the prize and never removed their eyes from it.

My niece was just like that, and I had another niece who had her eyes on the prize and was still able to be focused on other things, but knew exactly when to get back in the race. She was very successful and landed a top job with United Airlines in her junior year of college. Her position was to determine how much your airplane ticket would cost. She had that job at 20 years of age because she attended the 8th top school in the nation. She graduated from college at the age of 20. She has flown to over 25 countries. Every weekend, she was asked to fly to a new country until the Coronavirus pandemic broke out in March 2020.

Now back to what I was saying. I had the traditional students and taught them traditional math. They were so in love with me, and I was in love with them. Every class had a certain place in my heart and vice versa. I wasn't just teaching math all day, every day for 35 years; that would lead to me feeling burned out. I was over most of the extracurricular activities, which made my job easy and offered excitement. God gave me other talents such as: presenting and writing plays, teaching, singing, dancing, speaking, traveling, working in the community with the students, passing out baskets to the needy and elderly, and hosting special holiday presentations to the parents. I had the gift of bringing the best out of most of my students, especially the ones who were bashful or had insecurities. A lot of my students never had the opportunity to speak on a microphone, not to mention, in front of an audience. Once I worked with my students, built their self-esteem, and kept telling them, "You can do it," "You got this," and "You are ready to speak in the White House." They would blush so hard and get excited and tell me, "I never had anyone who believed in me or pushed me until I could do the task that was put before me." I would tell them how to stand, look all around your audience as you speak, do not speak in a monotone voice, project your voice, and sound the endings of your words. Speak with dignity and pride. Hold your head up and have good eye to eye contact with your audience. Speak distinctly and breathe. Never run on with your words. Take your time, speak, and breathe. Do not use your everyday voice but use your speaking voice to connect with the audience. Make sure their eyes are on you and that they're attentive.

I was not a singer, but I taught my students, who could sing, how to belt out their voices and sing with harmony. I taught them everything I learned at church and school. I was a most noble thespian in the glee club and drama club. I did a lot of acting and singing when I was a youth in my church. That gave me courage, tenacity, perseverance, and fearlessness. I was in many oratorical contests that my mom entered me in. She wrote many speeches for me and taught me how to articulate and pronounce words. I passed everything on to my students and more. I had a passion for everything I did, so I did it well.

My principal was a lady who admired me for all of my talents, and I did not mind sharing and instilling them in my students. I spent long hours after school doing those kinds of things at ease. I had no one to rush home to because my husband had just left me during this time. My career was booming and glorious, but my marriage was on the rocks and gloomy. Nobody knew it because God covered me through my talents, personality, good attitude, God-given smile, and patience with my students. One of my friends told me I was the only one he knew that can shine through a blizzard. Some things that people say to you, you know it is nobody but God. That really spoke volumes to me and kept me encouraged.

Chapter 6

My Shared Husband (God) Taught Me Everything

Even though God was shining through me on the inside, the human side of me was screaming, "Nobody knows the trouble I've seen." The marriage that I thought would last through thick and thin, through sickness or in health, was defunct. The man who promised, proclaimed, and took a vow in front of hundreds of people, told me he took me to be his wife, to have and to hold from that day forward, for better, for worse, for richer, for poorer, in sickness and in health, to love and to cherish, till death do us part, according to God's holy law, was no longer there. When we got married, I was an excited bride. Little did I know, my marriage would one day be in shambles, like many other marriages. I asked my mom innocently, "Did God really ordain marriage?" She told me that He did, and that's why Satan attacked it so. Even though Satan came in with fire sword feet and attacked my marriage, I never wanted to turn my back on God or throw in the towel. This was my chance to learn and know God for myself. Would He actually be my rock in the weary land, my joy in sorrow, my hope for tomorrow, my peace in the valley, and lily of the valley? Would He give me beauty for my ashes, the oil of joy for mourning, or the garment of praise for the spirit of heaviness? I really wanted to know would He answer me before I called, but most of all, I wanted to know and I wanted it to be manifested that God was my husband, as it is written in Isaiah. He did prove to me He was my protector, provider, counselor, and my friend. God showed me He was the lover of my soul, and that He is the only one that can complete me and never disappoint me. I realized that the God of this universe who knows all my flaws, my failures, worries, and weaknesses, still chooses to love me and call me His bride. "For the Maker is thine husband, the Lord of hosts is his name." Isaiah 54:50

I have learned during my walk with God that when everything else fails, try Jesus. God says, "For I know the thoughts that I think towards you, saith the Lord, thoughts of peace and not of evil," plans to prosper me and not harm me, "to give you an expected end" hope and a future. Jeremiah 29:11 Through my career, God was with Aretha. "And the Lord was with Joseph and he was a prosperous man." Geneses 39:2a

I appreciate Him for saving me and setting me up in life, leading me to the right career, and blessing me in my career. I had so much flexibility as a math teacher; I could choose the schools I wanted to work in and leave when I got ready. God had it planned this way on purpose for me. It wasn't about me teaching math, it was about me proclaiming His Word and being a living epistle for Him. "Ye are our epistle written in our hearts, known and read of all men." 3 Corinthians 3:2

When I see my students whenever I'm out and about, they always ask me, "Are you still teaching the Bible?" My eyes would well up with tears. I really did not recognize why it was so easy for me to transfer from school to school whenever I got ready. Wherever I would go, I would always get a warm reception basically with everyone. I was treated like a celebrity. "And the Lord was with Aretha." I thought it was because of the shortage of math teachers, but when I look back, I realize most teachers did not want to go from school to school. They wanted to go to that one particular school and retire from there in 30 years. It was their comfort zone. They knew their co-workers, the principals, the staff, the community, and the students. They knew what to expect, so contentment was acceptable. Some people do not make friends well, and some people just hate to deal with changes. God had made me totally the opposite. After two to three years, I wanted to have a new route to work, a new principal, new co-workers, new colleagues, a new building, a new atmosphere, and new students. As one of my brothers would often say, "It is good to see how another man eats his hamburger." I am a people person, so it was very easy for me to meet and greet people. When I went to a new school, I had so much to offer besides just teaching math. When students find out that you are a coach or a sponsor, they think you're pretty cool. This is always a plus, especially since you are one of the new kids on the block. Your gift will make room for you and bring you before great men. Students do not act out as much if you are one of the two, because they know most of the students respect you and the administration really has your back. After all, you are going beyond the call of duty without pay.

I do know I never neglected my church services nor did I ever say, "I am tired, I will go next week." During my 35 years of teaching, I only missed church when the doors of the church were closed or I was out of town. There was a time I called the pastor and told him that I was not coming. I was on the floor balled up like a fetus in so much pain. It was that time of the month for me. My pastor said you must be awfully sick because you are here every time the doors are opened. I received a phone call from an evangelist from California. She said God told her to call me and pray for me. After she prayed for me, she told me to get up, put on my clothes, and go to church. I knew that was God because I did not tell her that was my church night, nor did I tell her I had called the pastor and told him I was not coming. I was glad to get up and go to church. I sure was going to work the next morning. I know God is a jealous God, and Jealous is his name. "For the Lord thy God is a consuming fire, even a jealous God." Deuteronomy 4:24 "For thou shalt worship no other god, for the Lord, whose name is Jealous, is a Jealous God." Exodus 34:14 "For the Lord thy God is a jealous God among you lest the anger of the Lord thy God be kindled against thee and destroy thee from off the face of the earth." Deuteronomy 6:15

Sometimes when you have already told your pastor that you will not be in attendance, and he gives you an okay, that will be that on that. Regardless of whether you felt better or whether you have a purpose in your heart, you will still go to work the next morning. God sees that and he knows that, and He will do something about it because He is so jealous. God has done too much for us to make Him second fiddle or say, "I'll just get to Him when I get to Him." I found out that in walking with God, that only what you do for Christ will last. "And the world passeth away and the lust thereof, be he that doeth the will of God abideth for ever." 1 John 2:17

Happiness and richness come from the degree of your relationship with God. God sets limits to everything we go through, be it good, bad, or ugly. "For in Him we live, and move, and have our being; as certain also of your own poets have said, For we are also his offspring." Acts 17:28 God takes care of his own. Be not dismayed whatever betide. God will take care of you. Sometimes in life, I did have a loss of courage and a feeling of defeat. I can truly say that God did take care of me. God let me know, if you keep seeking me, I will keep covering you. Someone told one of my close friends, "I heard Dr. Terry was married to a lawyer who is always busy, but he really takes care of her." I was married to a lawyer in the courtroom, a doctor in the sickroom, and "He is the greatest friend of all, have you heard?" "For thy Maker is thine husband, the Lord of hosts is his name, and thy Redeemer, the Holy One of Israel." Isaiah 54:5a

God will be a father for the fatherless and a mother for the motherless. He will be your bread when you are hungry. He will be your water when you are thirsty. God has many names and will be what you need Him to be if you have a relationship with Him and walk with Him daily. This is not something I heard or something I read. I know this first hand. I have experienced and I am still witnessing the sure mercies of David. "I will make an everlasting covenant with you, even the sure mercies of David." Isaiah 55:3b God is so faithful and a promise keeper. God is not slack concerning His promises. "The Lord is not slack concerning his promises, as some count slackness, but is longsuffering toward us." 2 Peter 3:4a

Well, it was time for me to leave that school and do my next assignment for God. I was His ambassador. The school that God assigned me to went a little differently than my previous school. One of my principals was in the midst of a separation from his wife. He came to my church and was so encouraged. Another teacher had lost her faith, and she came to my church and was encouraged. The cafeteria manager was following the Lord afar off. I got the chance to witness to her and give her hope. The building engineer was leading a double life in terms of righteousness. I was a big inspiration to him. I did a quick work for the Lord in one year, and I departed. The Lord strategically made me a math teacher on purpose. There was always a math teacher shortage, locally and nationally. I did not realize it at first because I had so much favor in all my schools, but the Lord spoke to me and let me know I was in the right career. I was chosen to do mission work for Him. What one does speaks louder than what one says. "I thought on my ways, and turned my feet unto thy testimonies." Psalm 119:59

The only way some people will know and see Jesus is through the Jesus in me. Now that I have retired and have turned the page, I am very elated that God chose me for the task, and He could trust me wholeheartedly. I know a whole lot of people will say, "I know God called me." That is so true for the most part. The invitation of the gospel is preached to the whole world and reaches many. "Esaias also crieth concerning Israel, Though the number of the children of Israel be as the sand of the sea, a remnant shall be saved." Romans 9:27 The reason being is because the chosen are those who respond effectively with the true faith to call, that is why the scripture says, "For many are called, but few are chosen." Matthew 22:14 The point is that everyone has ears, but only a few are listening and responding. Not everyone who hears the gospel receives it but only the few who have ears to hear. The "many" hear, but there is no interest or is antichrist. Many are called and invited to the kingdom, but none can come on their own. It takes God to draw the hearts of those who come, otherwise, they will not. "No man can come to me, except the Father which hath sent me draw him, and I will raise him up at the last day. It is written in the prophets, And they shall be all taught of God. Every man, therefore, that hath heard, and hath learned of the Father, cometh unto me." John 6:44-45 I can stand flat-footed and say that my career, living, teaching, and preaching were not in vain, and up the road, I am looking for eternal gain with my crown.

Throughout my years of teaching, I learned that students are a product of their environment and I knew and recognized it. I could always tell the difference when a student was raised by a single parent that was working as opposed to a single parent that was not working. There was also a difference in the students who were raised by their grandparents. Over the years, I could discern the differences. Most of the time, when a parent of my students would come and visit me, God would let me know who the parent was, even though I had never seen them before. During my 35 years, God was using me as a vehicle to carry the Word. I did not realize it until halfway through my career because it was easy, natural, and the students loved my relationship with the Lord.

During the time I had a Pentecostal male principal, he gave me a welcome like no other principal. He called the entire student body and teachers to the auditorium to introduce me and asked me to stand. He told them my name and what I would be teaching and sent us all back to class. Other teachers had come, and he never gave them that introduction. He would just introduce them at the faculty meeting. God really exalted me that day. I worked under him for about two years until he was promoted, but while there, he didn't say much to me anymore, just in passing. He would be cordial but not friendly. He would always acknowledge me in taking off for the Holy Convocation and would give me the entire week off. He would say, "I saw you on TV." I had favor with him, but distant. He was promoted to another school and they replaced him with another principal. This principal was new and inexperienced and wanted to make sure everything went out right under his auspices. He allowed me to get a trip together for the students to travel to New York. I made a mistake and did not turn the money in on time. We had a policy that all monies of any kind must be turned in daily before 1:15 p.m. I did not follow that policy to the fact. He looked into it and saw that $720 was not turned in on time and told me to cancel the trip and refund the money back to the students. The parents, students, and assistant teachers were very disappointed and said he was prejudiced. I did not agree. Our school was always under scrutiny. He was a novice principal and was not going to lose his career over my negligence. Later on, he was promoted to a greater position. He would see me and felt bad about how he had handled that situation, but I would smile, letting him know that it was okay.

I knew my purpose and destiny in every school. I knew God was ordering my steps and directing my path. I knew nothing could happen unless God allowed it. From that moment forward, I carried my students for the next 12 or 13 years to New York. I went so much; I did not need an itinerary. I would go to New York two to three times a year, exposing friends and other church members, who would not have gone on their very own. New York is so big and has so much to offer. New York is a melting pot. The people in New York enjoyed my southern students, and they had favor at the restaurants and museums.

I remained at Mallory for an additional five years, under a white female principal, who was about four years older than me. God gave me unmerited grace with that principal. She made me Freshman advisor, and the sky was the limit for me. Whatever I suggested or needed, she gave me carte blanche. I was in charge of the Black history program, Thanksgiving, Christmas, Freshman Week, Winter Ball, dances for fundraisers, graduation, and trips to New York during Spring Break. She said, "I wish I had 10 Aretha Terrys." I looked forward to going to work every day. This went on for all of the years I was there. The students would come to me for everything. When it was time for the school calendar to be made for the next year, the principal and committee would check with me first. I had so much favor. I was a newlywed with no children, so teaching was cut out and designed for me because I had all the time for extracurricular activities; I could stay at school well beyond school closing time. "I was the head, not the tail, above and not beneath, I shall lend and not borrow." Deuteronomy 28:12-13.

Well, my career was at its highest peak. Everybody knew my name, and everybody was calling my name. My career was going up and my marriage was going down. My husband was a quiet man, so he did not do a lot of talking. He would tell me periodically, "Aretha, you talk to me like I am one of your students." I heard him and did not hear him because he would never elaborate or go into details, so what he said was meaningless to me. I knew his mom never cared for me the day I walked down the aisle with her, "mama's boy," but I had accepted it. Like I said earlier, I was on top of the world. I noticed my husband was distant from me. I saw and didn't see. I felt and didn't feel. Where I spent most of my time, I was "Queen Aretha," not "Queen of Soul, Aretha," but "Queen of Mallory."

I would constantly go back and forth to New York, asking my husband every time if he wanted to go with me, and his answer was always no, with no reason. Again, I would go with those who made me feel like a queen every day. Unknowingly, my husband had made up his mind to leave me. Again, I was going out of town with other teachers to tour five cities in Florida, with all expenses paid. In return, we will bring our students there on Spring Break. Yet again, I would ask my husband to join me. He would tell me to go on and enjoy myself.

I felt the distance in my marriage, but everything else was going my way. We had just gotten married and were learning from each other, and we were never intimate until our honeymoon. I knew a whole lot of adjustment would have to take place when we began living together, but nothing like this. He would tell me on Sunday mornings to drive my car to church because he was leaving after Sunday School and would meet me for dinner. This went on for months. I did not like it, but what could I do? Oh well, my marriage was on the rocks, but I was bigger than life on my job, so I didn't have time to talk about it with my parents or my best friend. My husband would take me out to dinner with two other couples on my job almost every Friday for two months. Then one day, a prophetess came to me and said, "The Lord said, 'Do not go out with those couples anymore.'" I just couldn't believe that, because this was the one thing my husband seemed to enjoy doing with me. So Satan told me, God did not say that, she is just jealous. I knew in my mind that God said it, but I just could not believe why He would say that. I'd rather obey if it wasn't God than to not obey and it was God and made a shipwreck. The couples enjoyed us, and my husband enjoyed them, but I remembered the prophecy. My husband would work overtime, so I used that as an excuse. My husband asked me what happened, and I told him we would do something else by ourselves. Days went on, weeks went on, and months went on. I took another trip without my husband, once again, after asking him to go. He told me again, he did not want to go, even though those couples we had dinner with would be on the trip, too. He told me to call my dad to pick me up when I got back. That sounded strange. On the day I got back to Memphis, I called and called, but he would not answer or return my call. Finally, I called my dad to pick me up, and he did not question me. When I got home, I was devastated. He did not call or touch base with me. I did not hear from him for several days. I called his father, and he told me to wait 24 hours and put a search out for him. In the back of my mind, I felt they were in this together. It did not matter. Reality had kicked in. He was gone, but he had left everything, clothes and all. I knew he would be back.

My father called a three-day shut-in for the members at the

church. This is where members would spend the weekend with Christ. I joined in with the members. That way, I would have strength from the saints. We stayed in the church, refraining from food and water. Just showering, consecrating before God, with singing, praying, testifying, and different ones expounding on the Word of God. I needed that. That shut-in timing was perfect for me. Strength for me. Peace for me. It sustained me. If I had stayed home, Satan would have beat me up and made me feel bad. "I was glad when they said unto me, let us go into the house of the Lord." Psalm 122:1 "God is our refuge and strength, a very present help in trouble." Psalm 4:1 "When thy heart is overwhelmed, lead me to the rock that is higher than I." Psalm 61:20 That Rock is Jesus. They always told me the church is the saint's hospital. I went straight to the ICU (the altar at the church, the front row). I did not sit in the back of the church, with my head down, saying, "Woe is me."

School was out for the summer. I locked myself up with the saints, attending the prayer meetings: Mondays, Wednesdays, and Fridays. I was so encouraged and was building myself up in God. Then God spoke to me and told me to get in my secret closet at home and go to the prayer meetings only one day a week, but pray every day with him. That was one summer that I really wanted school to open soon. August could not come fast enough. I had it all figured out, or so I thought, about what I was going to do each day when I got off work, so I would not miss my husband. School got out at 2:15 p.m., so I will make it home by 3:00 p.m. I will eat dinner and look through the mail until 5:00 p.m then look at the news and watch Bishop T. D. Jakes from 5:30 p.m. – 6:00 p.m. I would get my clothes out for the next day from 6:00 p.m. – 7:00 p.m. Normally I would get all my clothes ready on the weekend for the entire week. Since my husband had left, I needed something to fill my time in during the evening, so I would not miss him. While I was trying to figure out my schedule and timing out each day, God had things already lined up for me. My dad told me I could come back home. Then he said, if you do not want to come back home, just come and eat dinner with me and your mother every evening. All that was pure love that a dad had for his abandoned daughter. I said no thank you to both offers. I knew that was not the way the Lord wanted me to go. God wanted to use me in this test and through this test. God was now my husband. "For thy Maker is thine husband, the Lord of hosts is his name." Isaiah 54:5 "For the eyes of the Lord run to and fro throughout the whole earth, to shew himself strong in the behalf of them whose heart is perfect toward him." 2 Chronicles 16:9

I went over to my best friend's house, and my mother called me while I was there. Cell phones were not out then. My mom asked me to come to her house when I left. When I got there, my dad asked if his sister could come and stay with me. My aunt had just lost her husband from an illness. At that point, I was glad for almost anybody who was independent and not in my business. My aunt and I were already close from going to church together, so I responded with, "Yes." I asked my dad when she wanted to move in and he said empathetically, "Tonight!" I said that would be fine and he moved her in that night.

She would be so happy when I came home in the evening, and I would be happy to come home to her. She would cook, we would eat together, and she would clean up the kitchen during the week.

I would fry fish and fix baked potatoes with slaw on the weekend. We would listen to Bishop T. D. Jakes and enjoy ourselves. She never asked what happened or where my husband was. We went to church together twice a week. We were each other's earthly companions. Then she started looking for her own apartment at a senior living facility. They told her they would not have an opening until the Spring of the following year. Meanwhile, she enjoyed living on the river with me in my condominium. "And we know that all things work together for good to them that love God, to them who are called according to his purpose." Roman 8:28 She said she was glad to learn how to use the elevator, go to the laundry room, and use the washer and dryer. She learned how to live with other people in the same building and how to go to the mailroom and get the mail. She said those three months gave her strength and encouraged her to live by herself among other people in her senior living quarters. Walter Peyton said, "We are stronger together than we are alone." Reality had kicked in for me, too. Now I will have to run my house by myself, pay all of the bills, and make all the decisions. I had to really lean on the Lord and wait on Him. "Wait on the Lord, be of good courage, and he shall strengthen thine heart: wait, I say, on the Lord." Psalm 27:14.

Even though they told her that her apartment would not be ready until the spring of the following year, it was ready in three months, because God had plans for her life, and He had plans for my life. She stayed with me from August until the end of November. God wanted me by myself, so He could put me in His school and I would draw nigh to Him. "Draw nigh to God and He will draw nigh to you." James 4:8a God had already told me to get up early and pray before I went to work for an hour. I kept putting it off. He told me this on the first week of November 1994. I said I would start after the Holy Convocation ended. Then I said when my aunt moved out. Finally, I started praying before I went to work each morning for an hour around the 14th of November, 1994.

"O God thou art my God; early will I seek thee." 63:19 "I love them that love me and those that seek me early shall find me." Proverbs 8:17

I see why Satan did not want me to pray for an hour before I went to work. So many doors began to open for me. The students were well behaved, respectful, graded papers for me, tutored other students, they would go and get my lunch for me, parents would buy my lunch, and students gave me gifts on Valentine's Day, Christmas, and Teacher's Appreciation Day. I was always celebrated. They would compliment me every day on my attire. I never had a sad or lonely moment. All the praises that I would get from my students and principals outweighed the loss of my husband. "To appoint unto them that mourn in Zion, to give unto them beauty for ashes, the oil of joy for mourning, the garment of praise for the spirit of heaviness, that they might be called trees of righteousness, the planting of the Lord, that he might be glorified." Isaiah 61:3

The Thanksgiving and Christmas breaks were over. We had now made it to the second semester of the school year. I never told anyone at work that my husband had left and only just a few of the praying people at church knew. One day, as I was walking down the hall, this beautiful young teacher said to me, "Mrs. Terry, it doesn't seem like you go through anything." I was going one way down the hall, and she was going the opposite way. My eyes welled up with tears and I said down in my soul, "Nobody knows the trouble I've seen." My husband had left and she said, it doesn't seem like I go through anything. God allowed her to tell me that to encourage me, even though I was in the biggest test of my life. "I am covering you," He said. "In thee O Lord, do I put my trust; let me never be ashamed." Psalm 31:1a "And hope maketh not ashamed; because the love of God is shed abroad in our hearts by the Holy Ghost which is given unto us." Roman 5:5

I continued to teach math, sponsor programs, take students to New York during the Spring Breaks, kept smiling, kept fixing myself up, and kept being nice. No one knew but God and me. Ever now and then, someone would ask, "How is your husband?" I would always respond, "He's still working long hours," which he was, so that was not a lie. I would pass by his job and see his car because he worked downtown, and we lived on the downtown riverfront. My principal would give me six days off for the Holy Convocation that would come to Memphis every year. The only thing that had changed concerning me was that my husband left with only the clothes on his back. The Lord did not let him take anything. I thank God I was a tithe and offering payer. "And I will rebuke the devourer for your sakes." Malachi 3:11a

I stayed at that school teaching longer than any other school. All my good days outweighed my bad days. I couldn't complain. Even though the sun had started shining, I was able to "Endure hardness as a good soldier of Jesus Christ." 2 Tim. 2:3 I was hoping and praying every day that he would return. He would call ever now and then to see how I was doing. One day, he told me he was coming over so we could sit down and talk things out. He came with a huge yellow legal pad with different topics for us to talk over and discuss. We agreed on some things. He left, and the next time I heard from him, he was in the hospital. My parents went to visit him, and they told me he was really sick. I guess he was torn between trying to please his mom and please me. When he got out of the hospital, he never said anything else about us getting back together or making up. I went on with my life, realizing "this is it." Live for God and be Holy. I knew the way of righteousness.

I stayed in church, that was my strength, joy, and peace. I will tell any and everyone, "When you are going through, stay in the CHURCH." That is the saint's hospital. Even when you are strong enough to come out of ICU, please stay in the church, because other storms and tests will come. You would have already built yourself up for whatever betide you. God will take care of you. He will not forget your labor of love. "For God is not unrighteous to forget your work and labor of love, which ye have shewed toward his name in that ye has ministered to the saints, and do minister." Hebrews 6:10

I was at Mallory High School from 1988 to 1997. The school was no longer going to be a junior high school, but a middle school. God allowed a little friction to come between me and my principal, who once said, "I wish I had 10 Aretha Terrys." My time was up and it was time for me to be a witness at another school. She had the principal of Normandy High to call me and ask if I would come and teach math there. I was glad to go because those students had just left Mallory Jr. High, and some of them would be going to Normandy High, and over half would be attending another high school. I went to Normandy High. I had so much favor there. The students already knew me from Mallory Jr. High. They were glad for me to follow them. I had favor with the principal and assistant principals, the secretaries, cafeteria managers and cashiers, the building engineer, and his staff. Once again, I was on top of the world. I started a group of young ladies called, "The Ladies Unlimited," which was a step team. My goddaughter would leave her job in the evening and come to Normandy High to teach the girls how to step like sororities and fraternities. That went over so big. I became very popular for sponsoring that. The teachers were so happy for that organization coming to their school. We would have invitations to other schools, the coliseum, and talent shows. The Lord blessed my goddaughter to teach them well. My principal gave me the keys to the school van, gave me the gas card, and even gave me keys to concessions so we could raise money for uniforms.

My husband what? My husband left me? What? So what? "It really doesn't matter to me now." The students had me so pumped up and using a lot of energy and teaching math until when I did get home, I was ready for dinner, shower, and a cozy bed. I did not have a lonely night because God was my stay. "They prevented me in the day of my calamity: but the Lord was my stay." 2 Sam. 22:19 The principal began to admire me a little bit too much, and I recognized the plot of the enemy. I gave him back the keys to the school van, the gas card, and the keys to the concession stand and finished that year on out and put in a transfer. God allowed that. My time was up there, after the first year. A good time was had by all. I knew that my destiny was to go in being a beacon of light, living holy, and showing love. God always gave me a sign to make my move. I was always able to do it because math was a subject that every student had to take, and math teachers were in demand. God made me a math teacher for divine purposes. It worked for 35 years. To God be the Glory. Normandy High was a beautiful school. The colors were orange, white, and navy. The students had lots of camaraderie with each other.

It was a school with a lot of sisterhood, brotherhood, closeness, togetherness, and affinity. Well, my time was up at that time. I left and went to Forest Jr. High. The school was small and dark, with a small staff, and a very small student body. Everybody seemed to be closely knitted. But I had just come from a big, bright high school, where everybody had a lot of energy. The atmosphere at this school was great, but too laid back. The teachers were very comfortable in their attire, so I wore a T-shirt and a jean skirt every day because it seemed to be the order of the day. I was not used to this kind of atmosphere, but I was going with the flow.

The principal was very outgoing; he didn't care anything about his appearance or his attire. However, he loved his job, students, and community. He had lots of energy; he had two great counselors, but as I stated earlier, the teachers were laid back in their personalities and their dress. One day, as we were having a program in the auditorium, the principal was standing on stage receiving the teachers and their students as they walked in. The teachers led their students in the auditorium to sit down, with no strict direction, and then they stood in the back of the auditorium. When I entered the auditorium, I led my students to the front, filling in all the seats, with no spaces or rows between them. I took it upon myself to have the other classes do the same, while the other teachers stood in the back of the auditorium and congregated. My principal was so impressed with me for taking the initiative to organize not only my class but all of the students. He said, "You have supported me 100% in terms of discipline in the auditorium, and you are new to our school. You were not standing in the back of the auditorium just looking around like the other teachers who have been here. You organized the students as they walked in and told them to come all the way down without skipping a seat." He told me that went a long way with him and that I made a difference in the school with my presence. From that day forward, he would call my name over the intercom, announcing me as being over some special event, program, or trip.

My self-esteem soared, even though my husband left me. My marriage was shattered, but in my career, I stood out as the drum major of the school. They would say, "I am going to get Mrs. Coleman-Terry to chair this program or carry this group of students on a field trip." You would have thought I was the only teacher in that school that had talent or experience with working with students. I was everything on the job and in the community, but a failure in my marriage. As Martin Luther King said, "It really doesn't matter with me now." I know some people who love me, who appreciate me, and who accept me as I am.

Soon things changed. The Lord spoke to me and told me to fix myself up like I would when teaching at other schools. I started wearing my fur coats, pearls, fancy church clothes, and high heels every day. The school got a new facelift. They put all bright lights in the hallways and painted where needed. This small school made a big 180-degree turnaround. I started to look forward to going to work every day. I made an impact and a difference in that school with everyone. I was happy that God led me there. He put a lot of sunshine back into my life. Even though my marriage was black and bleak, I never told anyone on my job. I just kept smiling and I kept teaching. I kept incorporating programs and pageants at school. Whatever I suggested or wanted to do for the students was approved without hesitation. The other teachers even started fixing themselves up by purchasing new wardrobes, and above all, they started wearing pearls and being more active. They supported to the best of their abilities. The librarian and the guidance counselor told me how I had made an impression on the school and the principal. The principal told me, "I really appreciate you and all you do for this school. You have everyone fixing themselves up and now wanting to be more involved. Teachers who wouldn't give me the time of day before, are now cooperating with me." He said, "I am going to 'Do My Level Best To Make You Happy.'" I tell you, the sky was the limit to what I could have for me and my students. I had more power than the assistant principal. God opened that door, and no man could shut it. I had an evangelist who would pray for me every morning, a covering, and a shield. I did not recognize it then, but later on down the road, it came full circle. God knows us and how much we can take.

I carried the students, year after year, to New York on Spring Break. I put them in the Christmas Parade. I started the student government. I did a Mr. & Miss Pageant and also a football homecoming pageant. My pageants would be like Miss America pageants. We would do big programs, photoshoots on the river, and leave in limousines. Even Channel 3 News would come and show parts of the pageant. My students and I were on top of the world.

God gave me beauty for my ashes. Losing my husband could not equal the weight of my gain in blessings. I was so consumed with my job and my local church, I did not have time to miss my husband. This school took off and did not look back. Whatever program we had was packed out by parents and the community. I had one parent who even sponsored several students to go on the trip to New York.

The principal gave me my own personal computer. He told the counselors, "I am going to give Mrs. Coleman-Terry her own personal computer." I was flabbergasted because I did not know anything about a computer, although I took two courses and made top grades in both. At that time, I had no interest. Computers were very limited in a school back then. Many other teachers wanted it so badly, plus they were all into computers and wanted one for their own personal reasons. I was more into getting the students prepared for holidays, graduations, and math contests. He wanted me to have the computer as a gift to thank me for all I had done. I took the computer, and the rest is history. Look at God encouraging my heart. "To appoint unto them that mourn in Zion, to give unto them beauty for ashes, the oil of joy for mourning, the garment of praise for the spirit of heaviness; that they might be called trees of righteousness." Isaiah 61:3

I worked at that school for two or three more years under his auspices. I had shown my best friend, who is also a prophetess, a picture of him standing with the homecoming court. If she tells you something, you can stand on it. She will tell you only what God says, no more or no less. "Behold, I am against the prophets, saith the Lord, that use their tongues and say, He saith." Jeremiah 23:31

"I have heard what the prophets said, that prophesy lies in my name, saying I have dreamed, I have dreamed. How long shall this be in the heart of prophets of the deceit of their own heart." Jeremiah 23:25-26 My best friend looked at the picture and said, "Aretha, your principal is in a lot of trouble." My heart was exceedingly sorrowful. I did not know what she meant. She said God did not give her any details, but I knew if she said it, it was God. That was October. Approximately two or three weeks later, the Board of Education told him to clear out his desk and not return.

We had a female assistant principal, who was very thorough in paperwork. She was not a people person and lacked communication skills. No one really cared for her, and I was not her cup of tea, but she knew I was good for the school, students, and the community. She never catered to me. "Now there arose up a new king over Egypt, which knew not Joseph." Exodus 1:8 She allowed me to carry the children back to New York because the trip was already planned before the other principal was escorted out. The children had a glorious time as before. One of the students had gone into a convenience store and purchased an alcoholic drink and snuck it back to the room, unbeknownst to me. The kids did not want to tell me they knew because they thought they would never get the opportunity to go back to New York. When we returned, one of the students informed the interim principal. No one told me about the incident going or coming back to Memphis. The interim principal called me into her office and questioned me about it. I answered proudly, saying I knew nothing about it and that no one informed me. She got so angry with me for no reason, as if to say, you don't have favor with me. In a very mean voice, she said, "I will not tolerate this behavior, and you will not do another trip!" I said, "Yes ma'am," and I left. School ended the very next month, and they were still looking for a permanent principal. "For promotion cometh neither from the east, nor the west, nor from the south. But God is the judge: he putteth down one, and setteth up another." Psalm 75:6-7

She worked the entire summer as interim principal. They told her she would be replaced by a new principal, and her assistant principal position would be replaced as well, and she would be sent to another school. She was already up in age and did not welcome changes easily. When the new assistant principal asked her how long it would be before she cleared her desk, she did not give her a response. They said she was so shocked, she acted as if she had gone into a coma. They had to move her things out and bag up everything. She was so distraught. She was going to remain as an assistant principal, but just not at that school. She was so mean and hateful toward me. It might have been because I had so much favor with the principal. Nevertheless, the scripture said, "Touch not my anointed, and do my prophets no harm. Psalm 105:15 In life it behooves each of us to do good toward mankind. "If it be possible, as much as lieth in you, live peaceably with all men." Romans 12:18 A new principal and a new assistant principal moved in and were getting ready for the fall school year. God gave me favor with them, as he had so many times before with previous principals.

This principal was a good old-fashioned Baptist deacon from Mississippi. He had already retired from the school system in Mississippi and came here to work for a few years and retire in

Tennessee. He was not as generous in terms of me spending money on the students. He was average, which I was very grateful for. He really admired the Christ in me. Every Wednesday during our faculty meeting, he would always open it up, by saying, "How are you doing little preacher girl or little wig-wearing girl?" He would say it affectionately, plus he knew I had a lot of long hair, but wore a variety of wigs. I don't know what he was going by or what he saw in me that made him call me a little preacher girl. I never discussed my religion or faith with him. It was just something he saw in me that he admired. "Let your light so shine before men, that they may see your good works and glorify your Father which is in heaven." Matthew 5:16 I did go on to receive my doctorate in ministry and minister's license. Now that I look back, he spoke it into existence, and he could actually see my light shining. "Ye are the light of the world, a city is set on a hill cannot be hid." Matthew 5:14

On my face, it was my light shining all the time. Later on, he asked if I would take over the extracurricular activities and special programs. I was in charge of the morning announcements and all of the school happenings. My career was definitely ordained by God. I was a blessing to the students and faculty, and they were a blessing to me. The principal and I basically had the same last name. His first name was even the same as my dad's. He was a very nice man and had a love for the students. But, he also had a dark side and terrible temper, and once he lost it, he was uncontrollable. His wife went through a whole lot because of his illness, the bad uncontrollable temper. Even though he had a great love for church and Sunday school, it was not easy for him to live and walk wholeheartedly for God because he wanted to enjoy both sides of the coin. "And if it seem evil unto you to serve the LORD, choose you this day whom you will serve; whether the gods which your fathers served that were on the other side of the flood, or the gods of the Amorites, in whose land ye dwell: but as for me and my house, we will serve the LORD." Joshua 24:13

Living for God is a made-up mind. We cannot straddle the fence. "So then because thou art lukewarm, and neither cold nor hot, I will spue thee out of my mouth." Revelations 3:16 "Good understanding giveth favor, but the way of transgressors is hard." Proverbs 13:15 I have always wanted to live the life rather than talk about it. Anybody can quote scriptures. Anybody can say, "I know the man." But can you actually live the life? My philosophy is, turn your feet in the way of your testimony. Well, I left that school after the principal there gave me a going-away party and a scrapbook, and I was sent to Las Vegas for a seminar. Shortly, after two years, he left.

The school I went to was one of the high schools I had taught in earlier in my career. This time, I had a female principal who was a sorority sister. God gave me extra favor with her, which had nothing to do with our sisterhood. She told me when she interviewed me that she was going to interview several others after me. She told me to go on and sign the papers because everyone had spoken so well of me. "Art thou he that shall come, or do we look for another?" Matthew 11:3 So, the new school year had begun. I was excited about going back to one of my old schools. Everybody welcomed me back warmly. The new principal would stand in the hall with us each morning to welcome the students as they arrived.

One day, the principal said, "I am so tired of them bringing me breakfast from the cafeteria. I do not eat everybody's cooking. I just let it sit there on my desk." I immediately said, in front of the other teachers, "I will eat it!" She exclaimed, "Good, you can have it!" I told her I would come and get it every morning, but she told me she would bring it to me instead. Look at God. Favor is not fair. She would bring it each morning with the juice and all, just like she said she would. One teacher, that she was so close with, began to get jealous and made up a lie on me like Potiphar's wife told a lie on Joseph. My principal's whole personality changed noticeably towards me. She even stopped bringing me breakfast and became very distant and would throw out wisecracks toward me, which made me very uncomfortable in faculty meetings with my colleagues. It is good to know the scripture, which always encourages me, and that nothing happens unless God allows it. "For the Lord God will help me, therefore shall I not be confounded: therefore have I set my face like a flint, and I know that I shall not be ashamed." Isaiah 50:7 "No weapon formed against me shall prosper, and every tongue that shall rise against thee in judgement thou shalt condemn." Isaiah 54:17a

My dad died, and the school's courtesy club really showed kindness toward me. An announcement was made twice a day about my dad, and they gave me a large sheet cake with the school's name and colors. I had already taken off maybe three weeks or more to get my mom situated. She and my dad had been married for 61 years. Spring Break came, and one of the church ladies told me the Lord said to send me to New York. Oh my goodness, that was my favorite city! So I definitely went. I also wanted to go to California where my nephew and niece lived, but I was uncomfortable with taking off for nine days to go. We all know that Los Angeles, California is not the kind of city you go to for two to three days. My principal permitted me willfully. I told her I realized I had been out a lot because of the loss of my father, and if she said no, I would understand. She told me to go and enjoy myself. If you are faithful to God, God will be faithful to you. "And whatsoever we ask, we receive of him, because we keep his commandments, and do the things that are pleasing in his sight." I John 3:22

Whenever I had the opportunity to travel with the girls' basketball team to New York, I felt as if everything was coming up roses. But once again, my principal listened to another colleague who told lies about me, and she fell for it. She turned all the way nasty toward me this time. The same way she went out of her way to make me happy, she went out of her way to make me unhappy. She would make little innuendos that were very negative concerning me and my faith. I was humiliated. But, God gave me the strength to endure hardness as a good soldier. After I went through my tests gracefully, the lady or teacher that lied on me was exposed and got fired. Then two or three months later, they told the principal to clear out her desk and not return. She was devastated and outraged. She was too weak to clear her desk of her personal pictures and belongings, so she just left them. Well, that is not how the story ended. The teacher that lied on me was sent to another school that she thoroughly hated and had to teach a subject she did not like. Later on, she was in a car wreck and paralyzed.

When the principal left, she did not tell anyone goodbye, not even her assistants. Later, she had an affliction to come upon her, but it seems as if she recovered. I ran into her at a restaurant, hugged her, and complimented her. I told her to stop by my table and give me her cellular number. She got out of that restaurant really quickly and quietly. I never heard from her to this day. "But whoso shall offend one of these little ones which believe in me, it were better for him that a millstone were hanged about his neck, and that he were drowned in the depth of the sea." Matthew 18:6 Oh how I could not wait until that school year ended.

An opening had come up in Business, and again, I applied and was hired. It was the number one top school in Memphis. When you taught at that school, you knew you had arrived. Well, the devil came through my former principal again, and she called ahead and tried to block me, by saying something negative about me. When I arrived at the school, the principal told me that he was not aware of my coming and the Board of Education made a mistake. I knew that was a lie and a conspiracy. What God has for me, it is for me. Nevertheless, the Lord moved that principal immediately from that school that very week. He left the top school in Memphis, and I stayed! If God is for you, who can be against you? When God is with you, you will always be the majority. It is so important to have a personal relationship with Him. You do not want to only have a membership or churchship with Him. If so, you are doing yourself a disservice. When you have a one-on-one relationship with God, you do not have to figure the situation out or even try to fix it. The only thing you have to do is keep praying. And while we are trying to figure it out, God has already worked it out. "Thus saith the Lord unto you. Be not afraid nor dismayed by the reason if this great multitude for the Battle is not yours, but God's." 2 Chronicles 20:15

Any uneasiness, shocks, surprises, disappointments, or setbacks, belong to the Lord. There are no panics in God, just plans. "Who is he that saith, and it cometh to pass, when the Lord commandeth it not." Lamentations 3:37 Jehovah has the final say.

At this school, I had an easier subject to teach, keyboarding. My new assignment was great. The class was small with only seniors who needed extra credit to graduate. My computers didn't make it to school until just before Christmas, so I had to create my own curriculum. A group of teachers would meet in the morning to pray fifteen minutes before school started, and they invited me to join them. It was so funny. They would gripe for about ten minutes, say little cuss words, and pray for the last five minutes. I thank God that I would have already prayed for an hour before work. We are told to pray in secret, not just to be seen by others. "But thou, when thou prayest, enter into thy closet, and when thou hast shut thy door, pray to thy Father which is in secret; and thy Father which seeth in secret shall reward thee openly." Matthew 6:6 Some would make the sacrifice and get there early when the heat was turned up in their lives. When God would cool the flames, they refrained from coming early to pray. I thank God we were taught to seek the Lord when things were going well with us and when things were not going well. Do not wait to call on the Lord when you are in trouble. "I also will laugh at your calamity; I will mock when your fear cometh; When your fear cometh as desolation and your destruction cometh as a whirlwind; when distress and anguish cometh upon you. Then shall they call upon me, but I will not answer; they shall seek me early, but they shall not find me." Proverbs 1:26-28

God really smiled on me. It ended up being a wonderful year. I even did the address for the senior class during senior week. I started a little club after school and that led to an all-girls step team. I told them that I would be their sponsor and would meet with them two days a week. We would pray and do Bible study on Monday evenings after school and have step team practice on Tuesday evenings, and Chick-fil-A would sponsor our meals. That was my criteria, and the young ladies wanted me to sponsor so badly, and it worked out perfectly. We would receive so many invitations to city competitions and would receive 1st place everywhere we were invited because we put God in it and put Him first on Mondays. The students saw the difference it made. They will never forget that experience, and they learned it at an early age, the power of prayer, and when you welcome God in your personal life and personal situations, things begin to happen for your good. "In all thy ways acknowledge him and he will direct your paths." Proverbs 3:6

My girls received so many compliments and accolades for their hard work and character. They kept a 3.0 and above average for a whole year. They were exposed to the founder of "Build A Wall." She told them to build a wall around their virginity, and if they have lost their virginity, she told them to shut the door. "We have a little sister, and she hath no breasts, what shall we do for our sister in the day when she shall be spoken for. If she be a wall, we will build upon her a palace of silver and if she be a door, we will inclose her with boards of cedar." Song of Solomon 8:8-9 She taught them how to value their virginity very highly. She told them not to ever discredit the inestimable value of being able to present to their spouse their body and soul wholly undefiled and kept pure for their God-send-mate. The young ladies had many wonderful weekends learning how to be chaste young women. The workshops, plays, skits, seminars, games, and giveaways kept them wanting to come each time. It was simply splendid. They would have a great luncheon after each seminar. I was so glad for the exposure my girls received, and it was all Christian-based.

My purpose as a teacher was to teach various kinds of math and to prepare my students to score high on the SAT and ACT and attend college. My purpose on the spiritual realm side was to live a Christian life by precept and example. "I beseech you, therefore, brethren, by the mercies of God, that ye present your bodies a living sacrifice, holy, acceptable unto God, which is your reasonable service." Romans 12:1 God gave me an open door to spread the gospel through my life. Oh, how I enjoyed it. My students saw a difference in my life more than my other colleagues. I remember in one school that I taught in, six other colleagues were in my denomination, the Pentecostal faith. Some would always tell me, "There is no doubt about your faith, but I have questions about the other six." My principals would always let me take off six days with pay, and the other teachers had to bring in a doctor's statement after being away for three days. "A man's gift maketh room for him, and bringeth him before great men." Proverbs 18:16

God always gave me the liberty to speak and have favor with my principals. I thoroughly cherished those days and was appreciative for the doors God opened for me when there is a law of separation of church and state. The students had the right to lead and implement, but not the teachers. I thank God that the life you lead speaks more volumes than what you say. Anyone can talk a good game, but can you have it or incorporate the day-to-day lifestyle following and walking with God wholeheartedly? You have to be fully sold out to God and have a made-up mind to walk with God. When I say walk with God, it means that you completely change your lifestyle. The Bible says, "Noah was a just man and perfect in his generations and Noah walked with God." Genesis 6:9b Most times the only Jesus my students would see was the Jesus in me. I would ask the Lord to help me to be an instrument in His hand, the vehicle that carries the Word, an ambassador for Him, and a living epistle. "Ye are our epistle written in our hearts, known and read of all men." 2 Corinthians 3:2

I wanted my life to exhibit God's goodness, glory, and grace daily. I remember so plainly when I first started teaching, that I was ashamed for my students to see me reading the Bible. It was not a popular or cool thing to do at the age of 22. I would read the Bible, but I would have it covered up with my big math book. One of my students saw me doing this and made mention of it in the classroom. I was ashamed because I was a new convert and only had a little strength. "For whosoever shall be ashamed of me and my words of him, shall the Son of man be ashamed, when he shall come in his own glory, and in his Father's, and of the holy angels." Luke 9:26 "I know thy works, behold I have set before thee an open door, and no man can shut it, for thou has a little strength and has kept my word and hast not denied my name." Revelation 3:8

Because the Board of Education was phasing keyboarding out of the curriculum, I went back to teaching math. I left there and went to Klondell High School. I was low-key and very respectful. The students loved me as well. The principal was a math major and admired my math skills. He asked if I would be over the ACT club and teach calculus to the top 25 students of the senior class. I was so insecure about taking the offer because I never taught calculus before, so it would be very challenging for me since I would be retiring in a few years. But when I looked at my whole career, it was God who gave me the knowledge and wisdom to teach upper math, get access to students who were ready for the challenge, students who were only taking the course because it was a requirement for graduation, and students who had an innate ability for math since birth. It was God who allowed me to be a firm disciplinarian and be loved by my students. Math was already a difficult course to teach, and not being able to discipline, would have been another task. But, God gave me the victory over those giants' heads. My entire 35-year career was a faith walk, coming from a sheltered background laced with church, church, church. It took God to "Give me now wisdom and knowledge, that I may go out and come in before this people: for who can judge this thy people, that is so great?" 2 Chronicles 1:10

My niece told me she would come to Memphis over the Christmas break to help me brush up on calculus and give me some mini-lessons. What she did not know was that I needed an entire year to grasp it. "I can do all things through Christ which strengthened me." Philippians 4:13 After the Christmas break, I told the principal I would teach it. He was elated; the students were happy and like the scripture says, "For the eyes of the Lord run to and fro throughout the whole earth, to shew himself strong in the behalf of them whose heart is perfect toward him." 2 Chronicles 16:9 At the end of the year, these top 25 students of the senior class told me that I was the best math teacher they ever had. I gave all the honor and glory to God. "But thou shalt remember the Lord thy God for it is he that giveth thee power to get wealth, that he may establish his covenant, which he swore unto thy fathers, as it is this day." Deuteronomy 8:18 My faith has been increased and God is so, so faithful. I can remember the words of David saying, "When my heart is overwhelmed, LEAD ME TO THE ROCK that is higher than I." Psalm 61:26 I was LED TO THE ROCK so many times during the 35 years of my career. It drew me closer to God more and more. It also showed me who He is. Even though I was teaching students at school, I was being taught by the Master Teacher, God. I looked forward to going to work every day, and I enjoyed my subject, as well as my students.

Oh, the joy that flooded my soul during my career. Prayer is the key to everything and faith unlocks the door. God put me in a career where I had to seek him daily. "I love them that love me, and those who seek me early shall find me." Proverbs 8:17 "Every valley shall be exalted, and every mountain and hill shall be made low and the crooked shall be made straight, and the rough places plain." Isaiah 40:4

So my students finished the year with me in Pre-Calculus until their graduation day. They enjoyed me and discussed personal matters with me, while preparing for college and increasing their ACT scores. Graduation day finally came. It was a joy for me to see my 25 Pre-Calculus students leading the graduation ceremony; the Valedictorian, the Salutatorian, and the next 23 highest ranked. My heart was overjoyed to see my progress and the investment and bond that I shared with these students. I prepared them for the college days and the do's and don'ts as a freshman. I told them to hang out with students who are going somewhere in life. I told them, "boys and books" don't mix. You do not have to rush in having a relationship right now. I told them to focus on their education. As long as there is a world, you will have the opposite sex here on Earth. I told them to educate themselves and get all the education they can, while they are young, teachable, and don't have a family yet. "These are the best days of your lives."

There is one thing about teaching, you will see your students every day for 180 days until the end of the year. After that, some you will never see any more on this Earth. And ever now and then, you will see some who will still look the same. And on the other hand, you will have some come up to you and try to make you know them. Of course, by now, their appearance has changed because they have their grown-up look. Some will look older than you because the pressures of life have taken them down. Some can still tell you some of the things you taught them outside of math. Some will say, "Everything you told us then, I am telling my children now."

We had an end-of-the-year faculty meeting with an urgency. Everybody wanted to know what this meeting was all about. The principal met with us and said the targeted enrollment for the new school year was going down and they needed to lose two teachers. He stated that two could volunteer or else he would have to choose. Everybody got very quiet among 100 teachers and assistant principals. I said out loud, "I will volunteer." The room was so quiet and everyone looked at me with amazement. My principal said, "Dr. ACT, are you sure?" I said humbly, "Yes sir." I left there and went to Malone High School, where I was welcomed with open arms.

God would always give me favor when my assignment was up and it was time for me to move on to another school. "The steps of the good man are ordered by the Lord: and he delighted in his way." Psalm 37:23

I was under another Christian principal and assistant principal strategically ordered by God. I taught math and ministered to the students, such as was needed. One of the staff workers, who would eat free every day, gave me their lunch. That staff worker stated the school food was boring. Little did they know, that was my blessing and opportunity. "One man's trash is another man's treasure." That was definitely my treasure and money saved in my pocketbook. "Bring ye all the tithes into the storehouse, that there may be meat in thine house, and prove me now herewith, saith the Lord of hosts, if I will not open you the windows of heaven, and pour you out a blessing, that there shall not be room enough to receive." Malachi 3:10

The cafeteria manager always exclaimed that she liked me and admired my Christian walk, but she would charge me for every little thing. This other co-worker could get whatever they desired and more, and would not be charged one penny. So, God had that door open for me through that co-worker, who was tired of the food and thought it was boring anyway. I would smile real big. I was eating a full lunch, beverage, and dessert, if I desired all of that, every day. That was a fun, short year. I enjoyed the route I drove to work. It was very scenic and desirable, going and coming. I had to pass through the mall and the botanical garden. God has all kinds of ways to encourage your heart. I saw God in the big and small things. It was the small things that meant the most.

We had a big faculty meeting in February. The principal informed us that if the students did not meet the composite scores, the principal and teachers would be sent to other schools in the area. It was up to the Superintendent of that area who would go and who would stay. The Area Superintendent was one of my previous assistant principals, who did not particularly care for me because the principal at that time gave me much leverage. For no reason at all, he just did not like me. We did have a little run-in over the concession stand. I was over the concession stand and that particular Friday evening, the assistant principal told me to leave the water running in the sink over a pickle jar, for the entire weekend, so that the pickle taste would leave. I was very reluctant in doing so. But, he was my superior so I obeyed him against my will. When we got back on Monday morning, my principal got wind of it through someone who had gone in there first and reported it to the principal. The principal confronted me in front of the assistant principal. I looked at the assistant principal for him to reply. He stood there, about 6'3 and 275 lbs., and did not open his mouth. By that time, I was furious. I said, "This weak-kneed, jelly-backed man told me to leave it running for the entire weekend. I did not want to do it, but I did it because he was my superior." The principal laughed at the remark. I did not remark like that to score, joke, or belittle him. I did not want the principal to lose trust in me. That is the only reason I spoke up and out. The principal questioned him, but he had very little to say. I left them there talking to each other. Ever since, he has not cared for me. Was I supposed to have stood there and acted as if I did it on my own? No, because I did not want to come across as unreliable with so many valuables in the concession stand. The assistant principal could have easily said, "Sir, I left the water running." And that would have been between him and the principal. I was not going to take the fall for something I did not do, neither did I approve of it. That was a terrible year for that assistant principal, the students took his walkie-talkie and cussed him out on it, and everyone who had a walkie-talkie would hear the defamed things they would say to him about his clothes and appearance. That was like 13 years later from when I worked with him as an assistant principal. This time he was the district superintendent, so he purposely had me transferred.

I left Malone High School and went to Cyclone Middle School. That was an experience for me. First of all, the students were very young and energetic. In middle school, you have to walk the students to all of their classes, lunchroom, restroom, and to the front of the school at closing. I did this for about six weeks. I quickly got away from there. My doctor gave me a doctor's statement, stating that was too much for me with my shortness of breath. So they sent me back to Malone High School. Whose report are you going to believe? "Who hath believed our report? and to whom is the arm of the Lord revealed?" Isaiah 53:1 Jehovah has the final say.

The Board of Education gave me three schools to choose from. I went back to the school where the area superintendent uprooted me from. Everybody was shocked and was so glad to have me back. It is not over until God says it is over. "What shall we then say to these things? If God be for us, who can be against us?" Romans 8:31 When you have God, you will always be the majority. I came back and he was demoted from a district superintendent to a high school principal. They were not able to find a replacement since the day I left. Sometimes, God allows us to go through some things to show you He is with you, and He is on your side. The devil thought he had won and gained the victory. But God. God gave me victory over that giants' head. To God be the Glory for the things He has done.

I was two years shy of retiring, and I wanted to go out with peace, which God had always blessed me with during my 30 plus years. I have learned over the years, people will tell you one thing and do another. Even in a marriage, a person will stand before God, the minister, his bride-to-be, family, and friends, and quote those vows, and their heart is far from it. We have to be led by God in all that we do, be it big or small. God knows best. He knows us better than we know ourselves because He made us in his own image. "Know ye that the Lord he is God, it is he that hath made us and not we ourselves, we are his people, and the sheep of his pasture." Psalm 100:3

I stayed at the school until God ended my term. Everything was going my way again. God is an awesome God. Then God gave me another assignment at another school. I knew God was in it all the way. I enjoyed the change of schools. It was like I was being celebrated in every school I taught in, and I knew that is not normal. That was the path God had for me, and God knows I basked in it. A lot of people dread going to work, especially on a Monday morning, and they are saying, "Friday cannot come fast enough." I looked forward to going to work Monday mornings and I enjoyed all the other mornings. I got up early every morning and prayed for one hour before I went to work, and I was loaded with daily favor. I did not have sad stories as other colleagues and workers had. "Blessed be the Lord, who daily loadeth us with benefits, even the God of our salvation." Psalm 68:19

Everybody who knows God, please, please stay with Him and get all the way up in Him. And those who are reading this book, get to know Him personally through your tests, struggles, and vicissitudes of life. The closer you get to God, the things, situations, and issues you are struggling with will seem so far away and dim. They will not always be on the table of your heart and mind. Whereas you used to share with your friends or family members your struggles, they will seem so small and minute. "Draw nigh to God and he will draw nigh to you. Cleanse your hands, ye sinners, and purify your hearts, ye double minded." James 4:8 The deeper you are in Christ, the less your worries and uneasiness can control your mind and snatch you from your peace.

At my next assignment and new school God sent me to, no one really cared for the principal. He had Napoleonic Syndrome and never wanted to talk to you one-on-one. He was very short and very sharp in mathematics. Anytime you wanted to ask him something, he would always say shoot me an email, regardless of how small the question was. God had me, covered me, and he just could not figure me out. He had great respect for me because I was a math major like him. I was not in any cliques. I was very friendly with everybody, but not a friend of one. I was a very strong disciplinarian with the help of God. He told me he admired it when he would pass my classroom and see my students engaged, and they were all involved with the high-tech college calculator. That was God magnifying me to him. What he said was the truth, but I give all the honor and glory to God for the things He has done. Every accolade, honor, respect, gift, and favor came from God and because of God, it was no goodness of mine. I am very aware of whence I came, my background, my education, and how I made it. I will never forget it, all the days of my life. Even while I am writing this right now, my eyes are filled with tears. I never would have made it through the thorns and thistles without the Big He, GOD. I had severe limitations in a lot of areas in my life, but God covered me with His wings. "He that dwelleth in the secret place of the most High, shall abide under the shadow of the Almighty." Psalm 91:1 "He shall cover thee with his feathers, and under His wings shalt thou trust, his truth shall be thy shield and buckler." Psalm 91:4

I took off 90 days FMLA. He was so concerned that I was not coming back. Sometimes it is good to be missed. He held things down for me and found me a good substitute teacher. I cannot remember anything that stood out spiritually while teaching at that school. Other than the time I helped a teacher choose another career she was more comfortable with, and I helped another teacher get closer to God, whose husband left her on New Year's night after service at church and did not come home. I befriended her, and she started coming to my church and brought her entire family. We are in touch with each other today, even though she lived in California for a few years. She is a principal now. She looks good and is doing good. She knows the old-fashioned way of living for the Lord.

I taught mostly all seniors who needed one more math class for graduation requirements. That was a wonderful year, a fun year, and a quick year for me because I would be retiring at the end of that year, December 2013. Oh, how God opened that door for me again. When you are about to retire, you want an environment where the students are less challenging and the math curriculum is easy. You would like to have a smaller classroom size, an easy way to commute to work, and your bank, grocery store, and restaurants all by your job. Well, that is exactly what God gave me during the last two years of my retirement. It was everything a teacher could dream of. I did not ask the Lord for these blessings, he just passed them out to me.

When you are a math teacher, you teach all the students in the school, because math is a requirement for graduation. We math teachers already know all our classes will be maxed out, regardless of what school you teach in. The Bible says, "If ye be willing and obedient, ye shall eat the good of the land." Isaiah 1:19 A math teacher normally teaches 35 students a period and has six math classes per day, which totals out to be 210 students per school year. Well, I want you to know that Jehovah Jireh, my provider, and Jehovah has the final say, saw fit to reward me because He did not forget me. "For God is not unrighteous to forget your work and labor of love, which ye have shewed toward his name, in that ye have ministered to the saints and do minister." Hebrews 6:10

The year I retired, I only had one semester to teach. I taught Geometry Plus to 10th graders and 1/3 of them were hearing-impaired. Those classes were designed to be small because of the hearing impaired. So, I had a teacher who did sign language and a teacher's aide. God surely blessed me during that short school year. A lot of the time, they wanted to teach and one would grade my papers every day. I had it "made in the shade." We all got along well. They had very good math backgrounds. One would always go get lunch as well. I did not have over 15 students. This was the ideal setting. The students loved them and were comfortable with them both. One of the aides had cancer and would miss quite a few days, but when she came back to work, she would hit the ground running. She would make up for the lost time. Meanwhile, the other teacher filled in the gap; she was worth two teachers. That year was a breeze for me. I never knew anything like this existed for a math teacher. Math is a core course, every student has to take several courses for graduation requirements, therefore, the average math class would always consist of 35 students, unless you are teaching upper-level math such as Calculus, Trigonometry, etc. I was always faithful to God and a very faithful church member, regardless of the weather. I realized after submitting my ways to God, He was my constant companion and was in full control of my life. I could always trust God in putting up the green lights to go, the red lights to stop, or the yellow lights to stand still in situations. I am completely sold out to God. My goddaughter always says that I am a radical for God.

That was a wonderful way to end my career: burdenless and worry-free. When we would go out for our monthly fire drills, the teachers would ask, "Where are all your students?" I was very reluctant about going outside with my students because I knew the other colleagues would be talking. After all, their classes were running over. Really, I could have taken my two small classes and made one class, since I had an interpreter and an aide. God did not want it that way. To God be the Glory for all He has done. He strategically hand-picked those particular subjects, Geometry Plus and Bridge Math for me: two new courses that were added to the curriculum for a requirement for graduation. "For the eyes of the Lord run to and fro throughout the whole earth, to shew himself strong in the behalf of them whose heart is perfect toward him." 2 Chronicles 16:9 God gave me an end of my career reward. That was like pay for no work. Who wouldn't serve a God like this? The interpreter would put the grades in the computer. Everything was going my way, all because I obeyed the man of God. "Behold, to obey is better than sacrifice." 1 Samuel 15:22c

My pastor had already told us the previous spring that we were going to have a summer camp. I had taught students for 35 years, and I did not want to be involved with students in the summer. That is a teacher's "me time." You basically have 2 1/2 months that you do not have to deal with or teach anyone else's child. I did not want to be over any activities, neither did I want to go anywhere near that summer camp or be involved in it for five minutes. Summer is what all teachers look forward to, to exhale, regroup, catch up in your own personal business, life, and just plain chilling out away from children. You know the Word says the ministry is in need of me. So do you please God or yourself? I understood I needed to have worked and served where the ministry needed me the most and that was with the children in the summer camp. So, I humbled myself, gave up my summer, and attended every single day the camp was in session. I'm the kind of church member, sheep, or follower, that whatsoever the pastor sanctions, I am with it 100%. The pastor always said that he always goes by the leading of the Lord. I always follow him as he follows Christ. The Bible says, "But in lowliness of mind let each esteem other better than themselves." Philippians 2:3.

That summer was so, so boring to me. I gave it my all and drove 54 miles roundtrip to play an intricate part. I gave my hard-earned money every time. "And the King shall answer and say unto them,

Verily I say unto you, Inasmuch as ye have done it unto one of the least of these my brethren, ye have done it unto me" Matthew 25:40 "And whatsoever ye do, do it heartily as to the Lord, and not unto men; Knowing that of the Lord ye shall receive the reward of the inheritance, for ye serve the Lord Christ." Colossians 3:23-24. "Obey them that have the rule over you and submit yourselves; for they watch for your souls, as they that must give account, that they may do it with joy, and not with grief, for that is unprofitable for you." Hebrews 13:17. So it was and so I did. Before I knew it, the summer was over and school bells were ringing for me to come to work and teach my 150 students. So I did, because it was my career, my livelihood, and above all, my passion.

That was the last year of my career. I did not have to complete the whole school year because I had so many sick days. The state told me I could have taught just one month and did not have to return after Labor Day, which is in September. Since my assignment was very simple, I had two other teachers to assist me, and I had the smallest enrollment that I had ever had during my 35 years of teaching. My passion for teaching was so great, I stayed until Christmas. I did not return the second semester after New Year's Day.

I was able to exhale in my career; before I met the BIG EXODUS. So, when December 20, 2013, at 10:20 a.m. came, the principal made a big announcement over the intercom. That was my last hour and last day of 35 years. The students came to say goodbye for the last time. My principal asked if I would stay until the end of the next semester. That was a big compliment as opposed to some other teachers, where the principal, parents, and students were glad to see certain teachers retire. What my principal asked me was like asking an expectant mother to carry her baby twelve months instead of nine. I loved my career, my job, and my students, but I would not have stayed for a few more thousands of dollars. Thirty-five years is enough of teaching someone else's child for 180 days out of a year. I retired at 57 years old. Twenty-two of those years were centered around my education approximately. The other 35 were total children's involvement, non-stop, until I heard the final school bell ring on December 20, 2013, at 10:20 a.m. GOD DID IT. I did not leave with a bad name, a scandal, or forced to do an early retirement as some others did. God kept me.

I got in my car and screamed to the top of my voice, the highest praise, "Hallelujah," all the way from driving out the parking lot to the street. I had to pass several of the school buildings, but it was a release of my spirit and my praise to God. I was praising the Lord for many things. First, that I was in a career that I had a passion for and a job that stayed in existence. I was giving God the highest praise, praising Him that I was never accused of going with one of my students in the classroom or on an out-of-town trip. I was never accused of stealing money from the concession stand. Never accused of taking the school gas card and filling up my personal car with gas. I was never accused of buying groceries for the concession stand for my home. I never got in a fight with a student or another colleague. I never got written up for being late for work, calling in sick, or leaving my students unattended. I was never accused of selling drugs to my students. I was never accused of my students selling drugs in the community for me. I was never accused of going with the principal, us breaking up and arguing and fighting, and being sent to another school. I was never accused of getting pregnant by one of my colleagues or one of my student's parents. I was never accused of carrying students to my home and having wild parties, involving sex and alcohol. I was never on the 5:00 evening news for anything illegal or negative. I did not go to work and there was a big lock on the door, whereas no one was notified about a closing. ALL of these things happened to many teachers during my 35 years. "Wherefore let him that thinketh he standeth take heed lest he fall. There hath no temptation taken you but such as is common to man: but God is faithful, who will not suffer you to be tempted above that ye are able; but will with the temptation also make a way to escape, that ye may be able to bear it." 1 Corinthians 10:12-13

That is the reason I was giving God the highest praise because it was God who kept me. I could not keep it to myself. The Lord can keep you because there is nothing God cannot do. God is never surprised or shaken. God made all things, sustains all things, and rules all things, including every detail of our lives. "Now unto him that is able to keep you from falling, and to present you faultless before the presence of his glory with exceeding joy." Jude 1:24 I can truly say that God is a keeper. If by chance you stumble or even fall, He is right there to pick you up because of His love. "The Lord is not slack concerning his promise, as some men count slackness; but is longsuffering to us-ward, not willing that any should perish, but that all should come to repentance." 2 Peter 3:9

I was praising the Lord that I was able to maintain my career until I retired. I did not have to choose another career because it had been phased out during my 35 years, or I had to teach at a designated school because the subject I was teaching was not needed. I had favor basically in all the schools I taught in, and in the community as well because I was involved in extracurricular activities. I was praising the Lord for the trips that I took with the students going to New York, Florida, Texas, Mexico, and Washington D.C. I never got in trouble for hitting a student or any little or big things that schools are experiencing with bad teachers' behavior. I was praising God I retired with dignity and with class. He had made me glad. "Ye are the light of the world. A city that is set on a hill cannot be hid." Matthew 5:14 "The Lord shall make thee the head and not the tail and thou shall be above and thou shalt not be beneath." Deuteronomy 28:13." "Thou shall keep him in perfect peace, whose mind is stayed on thee, because he trusteth in thee." Isaiah 26:3 "A good name is rather to be chosen than great riches and loving favor rather than silver and gold." Proverbs 22:1

My dad always told us to get a career in a field that we can retire from. Sometimes it is not about the money, it is about the stability of a job and flexibility. Being a math teacher, I was licensed to teach math, K-12. That gave me great flexibility, and I was able to find my niche, and that was high school students preferably 17-19 years of age. They were mature for the most part and were serious about graduating, so I always had a tool to hang over their heads. They wanted someone to look up to and confide in, which made it very easy in disciplining. I also learned along the way by going to church through the week, which really gave me a better quality of life. It enhanced my natural, spiritual, financial, physical, and emotional life. I can tell the things that other teachers were experiencing because I was experiencing some of them as well. I was able to cope and deal with it differently than they did. Some of them would be in the teacher's lounge boohooing about their problem. I would have the very same problems, but God gave me peace in the midst. "Mark the perfect man and behold the upright, for the end of that man is peace." Psalm 37:37 "These things that I have spoken unto you that in me ye might have peace. John 16:33a "Peace I leave with you, my peace I give unto you, not as the world giveth, give I unto you. Let not your heart be troubled, neither let it be afraid." John 14:27

That is why it is so important to stay in church and to hear the Word being proclaimed and explained. I have learned over the years, sometimes a song can be sung that can address what you are going through or give you the answer to hold on. Don't give up because "God is at the door." You can bask off that for a long time or even in the weeks to come. God knows exactly what everybody needs. He gives us the answers in so many facets. We just have to be available and capable to receive them. God is a gentleman. He is not going to make us come to Him. We have to have a sincere heart and a willing mind. "But without faith it is impossible to please Him, he who comes to God must believe that He is, and that He is a rewarder of them that diligently seek Him. Hebrew 11:6 Going to church was a divine prescription for me. "Not forsaking the assembly of ourselves together, as the manner of some is." Hebrew 10:23a

I gave myself a retirement party at the school, and I also gave myself a grandiose retirement dinner at the Hilton. I had all the bells and whistles. I had the R.O.T.C. Drill Team do a drill and salute as me and my family members walked in. I had two professional psalmists, a comedian, along with an actor. I had some of my former students, who were now successful young adults honor me with remarks. They included an attorney, an entrepreneur, a VP of Human Resources, and several others. They made me proud as they stated in their speeches how I was very influential in their successes. They presented me with flowers and gifts. It was a beautiful dinner with a buffet, music, and singing. All of my family members, siblings, and close friends flew in to make this a grand event.

My dad had already made his transition to glory, and the Heavenlies were beckoning for my mom. I am still thanking God for my parents and my grandmother, who taught us True Holiness by precept and example. During my entire life, my parents never wavered. They told us it was "Holiness or Nothing." "You can not walk straddled the fence." My dad told us when we liked it and when we didn't like it, "To seek the Lord," for everything. I found out that was and is the answer and key to life's problems and situations. We learned that "Seek the Lord" is praying every day when you first wake up and before you leave the house for any reason. We also learned to read His Word. We learned that when we pray, we are talking to God, and when we read the Bible, God is talking to us. "Logos" is God's Word that we read and when we go through a test, trial, or tribulation, then God will give us a "Rhema" Word that addresses our situation, that we have already read in the Bible. That is why it is so imperative that we read God's Word daily, so God can order our steps through "His Word." "For the Word of God is quick, and powerful, and sharper than any two-edged sword, piercing even to the dividing asunder of soul and spirit and of the joints and marrow, and is a discerner of the thoughts and intents of the heart." Hebrew 4:12

My mother would have family prayer just at the time we would be having so much fun outside with children from other streets in the neighborhood. We would be outside playing foursquare with a big round ball. Those were the kinder and gentler days. My mom was very protective; she would peek outside ever so often. Now that I am older, I realize that is why she would call us in when other big boys would come over and play from other streets. I just thought that was a coincidence, but she was constantly peeking out. We were very obedient. That was the way we were raised. We would get out of line and stop playing ball without questioning our mom. We felt like, "Mom knows best," even though we did not understand. Further up the road, we understood. Girls were getting pregnant, boys were drinking and getting high, but our mom put that fear in us at an early age and kept us in church every Sunday and through the week. That was not the kind of life that we wanted to lead. I can truly say, it kept us from a million failures, whereas, some of our other friends experienced life early and suffered many, many consequences from it.

We admired the freedom our friends had, but it took them down a dangerous road. They had so many pitfalls in life that we never had to go through or experience. We did not appreciate our parent's strictness, but we did not know any better because we were just children and wanted to look like everybody and do like everybody else. But, God forbade. Mom knows best, and Father knows best. When the parents fail, the children fail. When the parents promote salvation and education, most likely, the children will promote salvation and education. I did it all through my 35 years of my career. You know how when some people talk, every other word is a cuss word. Well basically, all my life I promoted education and salvation. My dad did most of the harping on education, and my mom and dad together harped on salvation in our lives. Oh, how that harping blessed my soul, my career, my friendships, working with others in the workforce, irate parents, wayward children, and a variety of bosses. We were not cognizant of the fact that what our parents were instilling in us would stick with us for life and would be our life guide. I doff my hat to my grandmother, mom, and dad. "Honor thy father and thy mother which is the first commandment with promise." Ephesians 6:2 This scripture has been displayed and exhibited over and over and over again. The promise is, "That it may go well with joy and that you may have a long life on the earth." Deuteronomy 5:16

In elementary, junior high, and high school, I was not one of the in-crowds at school. But God always shined a light on me in my own personal setting or career. My peers would always compliment me on my various gifts, talents, and my smile. They would always equate me with Aretha Franklin because I sang in the glee club, and my name was Aretha. Being in the glee and drama clubs gave me the experience to speak in front of people. I did all kinds of public speaking at church and was always entering oratorical contests. I was always in Christmas and Easter plays in church. These different talents and gifts broadened my horizons. As I stated earlier on, I was raised very sheltered, but by the same token, my personality caused me to blossom among my peers. I came across as being outspoken, not afraid to speak up and out, will talk to anybody, and was very quick to laugh and smile. I truly believe, because I participated in the church and school, I was the Spelling Bee Champion of my school. I was nominated Chaplain of the senior class and Miss Charm. The chaplain came about because I acted like and looked like a church girl; students just put two and two together. Miss Charm came about because I was always smiling. Now that I look back, those are gifts that were truly natural from God. God blessed me with that; something that my parents would approve of, and not going against their "status quo." God already knew before the foundation of the world, who I was and what I would become. "Even as He chose us in Him before the foundation of the world, that we should be holy and blameless before Him. In love, He predestined us for adoption to Himself as sons through Jesus Christ, according to the purposes of his will." Ephesians 1:4-5 ESV

On graduation night of my high school senior year, the class officials led the graduating class in the coliseum. I was one of the six, along with the Valedictorian and Salutatorian, giving their speeches to the masses. I was chaplain, so I spoke as well. God opened that door for me, "the little sheltered girl." "Ye are the light of the world. A city that is set on a hill cannot be hid. Neither do men light a candle, and put it under a bushel, but on a candlestick; and it giveth light with all that are in the house. Let your light so shine before men, that they may see your good works, and glorify your Father which is in Heaven." Matthew 5:14-16 All of the speaking occasions helped me not to have "stage fright" and how to speak in front of people, in front of my students, how to handle business affairs, deal with challenging people, and how to defuse arguments and disagreements. My parents were so instrumental in my life more than they ever knew. God did it through them. God has truly blessed my going out and coming in throughout my life. "The Lord shall preserve thy going out and thy coming in from this time forth, and even forevermore." Psalm 121:8 I have had over 20 bosses in my career, females, males, different cultures, some non-Christian, but through it all, God made me like a flint. "For the Lord God will help me; therefore shall I not be confounded, therefore have I set my face like a flint, and I know I will not be put to shame." Isaiah 50:7

My parents and I, along with my sister and her children in the 80s.

College Life

I started college right out of high school. I graduated from high school, May 1974, and started college, June 1974. I had to go that summer and take remedial college courses because I did not do well or score high on the ACT. First of all, I did not know the real importance of scoring high, I just thought it was just a plain entry exam to get into college. I did not know about low or high scores until I was well down the road. No one made a big fuss, like they are doing now. If you make a 21, the average college will accept you. If you make a 24, it places you at the 74th percentile, better than 75% of test-takers. If you have scored a 21, then you have scored higher than 50% of test-takers. The highest score is 36, anything 35 or above is in the 99th percentile and is truly a phenomenal score. Well, let me tell you what the Lord blessed me to make. Are you all ready for this? Dr. ACT, Dr. Aretha Coleman-Terry made a perfect 14. To God be the Glory. Like I said, there was not any emphasis put on it in my home. My older siblings who had gone to college, never put any emphasis on it or told me to prepare for it or score high. I was just told I was going to college and it was not an option. So, there I was sitting in summer college right before my freshman year, taking Remedial Math and English. It was a lot of fun. I learned a lot, made lots of friends, and it prepared me for freshman year holistically. "It's not where you start, it's where you finish.

My freshman year was a breeze. I worked at Kroger Store as a sacker and moved up to a cashier. I never missed a beat from work, school, or church. I went to church every Sunday, and we still had family prayer at home until our various work schedules caused otherwise. I stayed in church and paid my tithe and offering religiously. God was very faithful to me. I made very good grades and was a tutor for Statistics. I also did "work-study". I was financially set, living at home with my parents. My father gave me lunch money and bus fare to get back and forth to school. College life is what you make it. I did not have a personal relationship with God, but I stood in awe of Him. I knew right from wrong. I knew if I died, I was not going to heaven because God was not first place in my life, even though I went to church every week, participated in the church, served as Sunday School secretary, sang in the choir, and participated in several church plays. God still was not my main priority. It was my boyfriend and friends. I knew Holiness was right, but I just was not ready to live it. "Train up a child in the way he should go and when he is old, he will not depart from it." Proverbs 22:6 "While it is said, Today if ye will hear his voice, harden not your hearts, as in the provocation." Hebrew 3:15

I thank God for looking beyond my faults and seeing my needs. I also thank Him for having mercy on me, a sinner. "I was not fit to live and afraid to die," because I was unprepared to meet my creator. I had already made up my mind, that I was not going to be out in the world long. Church was written all over my face. I wanted to see what the world had to offer because I'd had chains on me all my life. Now that I was grown, I just wanted to see. Well, it was pretty cool and fun...the little things I did experience. Nevertheless, it was not worth me losing my soul. God made me for His purpose. He gave His only begotten Son a ransom for my life that I may have the right to the tree of life. I was purchased by His blood. I had to make up my mind about whom I would serve.

I kept the same two friends throughout my four years of college. We traveled together, my mother took us shopping together every pay period, we went out together, and we dined together. I only had two boyfriends during those four years of college. The first young man I met in high school. He was very generous, but very possessive. I broke up with him and started dating a young man who lived down the street from me. He was very nice and my family members admired him. He was eight years older than me. He was a joy to have and a good friend. We dated until I graduated from college and got my first job as a teacher.

In college, I was considered as one of the best-dressed students because I worked at the Bulk Mail center, which is a subsidiary of the United States Postal Service. I worked there and helped two of my other friends get hired through my uncle.

I had a great big graduation with my grandmother, father, siblings, boyfriend, and two best friends from childhood. My mother could not make it. She had flown to Flint, Michigan to be with my elder sister, who was having her first baby.

It was an exciting week for us all. My father bought me a chocolate-colored fur coat. It was something beautiful from Franklin Simon. I was so, so happy and blessed. God has always prospered and favored me from my youth up. God's hands have always hovered over me. My graduation day was Saturday, April 15, 1978. I was so happy about my Bachelor of Science degree. I was not thinking, looking, or asking for another degree, not knowing I would obtain my Master's degree, Plus 45 degree, and above all, my Doctorate. "But as it is written, eye hath not seen, nor ear heard, neither have entered into the heart of man, the things which God hath prepared for them that love him." I Cor. 2:9 When I accepted Christ as my personal savior and began to walk with Him, I began to receive the blessings of Abraham, Isaac, and Jacob. "That in blessing, I will bless thee, and in multiplying I will multiply thy seed as the stars of the heaven, and as the sand which is upon the seashore; and thy seed shall possess the gate of his enemies." Genesis 22:17

I have always been a generous person, and I always had favor upon my life since elementary school. During that time, I just thought people liked me. By going to Sunday School, Bible Study, and prayer meetings, I distinguished differently. I really learned about giving. I learned that giving incorporates the law of reciprocity, the more you give, the more you receive. "Freely ye have received, freely give." Matthew 10:8b "Give, and it shall be given unto you; good measure, pressed down, and shaken together and running over, shall men give unto your bosom. For with the same measure that ye mete withal shall be measured to you again." Luke 6:38 We all know that giving and receiving belong together. When we give, it puts us in the position to reach out and receive a harvest. We should have a spirit of expectancy. Your blessings can come from a low utility bill, gas prices going down near you, someone takes you to lunch, someone fills your car with gas, an unexpected check in the mail, or extra money in your bank account from the unknown. The unknown is God. Just so many showers of blessings. "And all the blessings shall come on thee, and overtake thee if thou shalt hearken unto the voice of the Lord thy God." Deuteronomy 28:12.

Our giving is not a debt that we owe, but a seed that we sow. I have always paid my tithe and offering from a child up because our parents told us to tithe off everything we received. They told me anything you do 13 times consistently, becomes habit-forming. Paying my tithe and offering is just like washing my face and brushing my teeth. It was a way of life. The more I gave, the more received, and it was very noticeable. Whatever I gave out, I would get that back and more. I never had a loss in giving, I always had gains. When I was young, I did not understand when the Word said, "It is more blessed to give than to receive." Acts 20:35 When we give, we take on the nature of Christ. Christ gave His life for us. "God commandeth his love toward us, in that, while we were yet sinners. Christ died for us." Romans 5:8 Giving is how God demonstrates His love for us, it makes you happy, it blesses others, it helps us to live longer, it's an act of obedience, it gives your life meaning, it increases our confidence, it builds trust, you live and see life differently, it brings contentment, it makes you likable, and it is a defense. "For wisdom is a defense, and money is a defense. Ecclesiastes 7:12

As a teacher, I had students from all walks of life. It depended on the school location and the neighborhood. I taught at two different schools surrounded by very large housing projects. Those students were very street smart and knew how to survive off so little. A lot of them became mothers at an early age. They were soft-hearted and hard-hearted. They wanted love, like all of us, but some obtained it from ways we thought were unthinkable. Some had positive outlooks on life, some mediocre, and some were definitely a product of their own environment. A lot of the generational curses were passed down. Some of my students would have four generations in one home: the grandmother, the mother, my student, and her baby. It would be a vicious cycle. Someone would have to break that cycle, and I did everything I could to instill a positive future. I would write on the board in all capital letters, MY PRESENT CONDITION IS NO INDICATION OF MY FUTURE POTENTIAL IN GOD. I would say verbally when I could, "You can make it in this world with SALVATION and EDUCATION." I gave out love every day in tangible ways, physical ways, and emotional ways. I would pick up some of my students and carry them to church with me. It really paid off. Some are ministers and elders, and when I see them now, they would thank me and reassure me that my teaching and living were not in vain. I knew teaching math and being certified was the open door for me to teach righteousness through my life and let them see Christ being exemplified. So many of my students were cussed out since they were babies because babies were having babies. For some, it was just a way of life and normal household language. I showed them unconditional love, whether they deserved it or not because love is unconditional. "And we have known and believed the love that God hath to us. God is love; and he that dwelleth in love dwelleth in God, and God in him." 1 John 4:16 "And we know that in all things God works for the good of those who love him, who have been called according to his purpose." Romans 8:28 "Love is patient, love is kind. It does not envy, it does not boast, it is not proud. It does not dishonor others, it is not self-seeking, it is not easily angered, it keeps no record of wrongs. Love does not delight in evil but rejoices with the truth. It always protects, always trusts, always hopes, always perseveres.

Love never fails." 1 Corinthians 14:4-8a

Love is an action word. I just didn't talk about it, I exemplified it in sundry ways; that made them gravitate to me. They also shared personal things with me, and I was able to give them counseling through the Word. This gave them a true foundation and something they could hold on to for life. Whatever is from the heart reaches the heart. "Keep thy heart with all diligence, for out of it are the issues of life" Proverbs 4:23

Sometimes, I run into some of my students, and they thank me for something I had either done for them or said to them. Sometimes I do not recognize the student because I taught over 8,000 students in 35 years and they were teenagers then. Now all of them are all grown with their spouses and children. It makes me feel great just to know I had encouraging words, was a positive role model, had time to listen, and exhibited love if sometimes they felt they were not. You never know what is going on in the home, what kind of parents they had, what the environment was like, did they have to fend for themselves, or were the mom's boyfriend bothering them. As you would know, I had three different young ladies from different high schools, where the mom's boyfriend was seducing them. Two of my young ladies were going with their mom's boyfriend, and one of my young ladies and her sisters were attacked by the biological father. It was reported the father was removed, and a few years later, the mother let him back in. Those girls were messed up emotionally and mentally. My student was not as damaged as her sisters were from the ordeal. "Confess your faults one to another and pray for another that ye may be healed. The effectual fervent prayer of a righteous man availeth much." James

5:16

When one has a persistent day-to-day prayer life, God gives that person great power and wonderful results. For some, the only Jesus the children would see, would be the Jesus in me. "Let your light so shine before men, that they may see your good works and glorify your father which is in heaven." Matthew 5:16 I thank God that He gave me a career in working with children and teaching them math daily. I was able to bond with them, love them, and be an effective role model, teacher, counselor, mom, nurse, dietician, sister, best friend, and sanctified minister. I remember my non-tenured year as a teacher, and one of my students was very distraught. She learned that she had cancer at the age of 16, and she asked me to pray for her. It was an honor to me because I was very young, fresh out of college, and inexperienced, but it was something she saw in me that she did not see in her other five teachers. I thank God for the faith she had in me and that increased my faith. I prayed for her and forgot about her and the situation because my focus and goal were to be an effective math teacher and a strong disciplinarian. "Is any sick among you? Let him call for the elders of the church, and let them pray over him, anointing him with oil in the name of the Lord. And the prayer of faith shall save the sick and the Lord shall raise him up, and if he have committed sins, they shall be forgiven him" James 5:14-15

I can truly say that the career that God gave me kept me on my knees, kept me in the Word, kept me fasting, and kept me in all the church services. Anytime you are teaching a hardcore subject like math to high school students, it doesn't matter how well you know the subject or the curriculum. What matters is how well you can get it over to the students. Math is the kind of subject that when some students immediately see it on their schedule, it strikes fear. Some students have been told by their parents, relatives, and friends, "I never did good in math", "Math was my worst subject", "I hated math", or "I never caught on in math." Some students come already with a defeatist attitude, "I can't learn math either" or "I know I am going to fail math." First, I had to win the student's confidence to ask questions, and then I had to enforce a comfortable learning environment. If they feel comfortable with you, then they are apt to ask questions until they understand. Therefore, I had to have a one on one daily prayer life with God. "In all thy ways acknowledge him, and he shall direct thy path. Proverb 3:6 "For in him we live, and move, and have our being." Acts 17:28. My career kept me in the Word. "Thy Word is a lamp unto my feet and a light unto my path." Psalm 119:185 "For the Word of God is quick and powerful and sharper than a two-edged sword." Hebrews 4:12a

I had to memorize the scriptures to encourage myself and to keep a true foundation. "But without faith, it is impossible to please him for he that cometh to God must believe that he is, and that he is a rewarder of them that diligently seek him" Hebrews 11:6 I would get up an extra hour earlier to have time to pray and read the Bible before I left for work. Yes, Lord, it did work. That was my spiritual prescription and my daily dose before I left the house. Regardless of whether I was going to work on the weekdays or if it was the weekend, I made sure that I gave God quality time because I found out it worked immensely for me. "I love them that love me and those that seek me early shall find me." Proverbs 8:17

God knows what to allow in our lives to draw us closer to Him and to depend on Him for peace. If everything was going well in our lives and all our ducks were in a row, we would not take the time to pray or talk to God because we would have the attitude, "We Got This." All of our tests come to make us better and not bitter. "Draw nigh to God, and he will draw nigh to you." James 4:8 God knows how to draw us through tests, trials, and tribulations. Every test we go through is tailor-made for us. It is not a one-size-fits-all. God knows exactly what it takes to keep us humble and He said He sets the limit, the severity of it, the timing, the beginning, and the ending. Sometimes we go through tests after tests. The good thing about it is, if we have a relationship with him, like the three Hebrew boys, Meshach, Shadrach, and Abednego, he will get in the fire with us, lighten the load, and cool the flames. The three Hebrew boys had faith in God and a personal relationship with Him, which gave them stamina and boldness. "Ye fall down and worship the image which I have made; well: but if ye worship not, ye shall be cast the same hour into the midst of a burning fiery furnace; and who is that God that shall deliver you out of my hands? Shadrach, Meshach, and Abednego, answered and said to the king, O Nebuchadnezzar, we are not careful to answer thee in this matter. If it be so, our God whom we serve is able to deliver us from the burning fiery furnace, and he will deliver us out of thine hand, O king. But if not, be it known unto thee, O king, that we will not serve thy gods, nor worship the golden image which thou hast set up. Daniel 3:15b-18 Whatever betide you, if you have a personal relationship with God, He said in His Word, "And it shall come to pass, that before they call, I will answer, and while they are yet speaking, I will hear." Isaiah 65:24 God loves and wants to prove

Himself strong on our behalf, so that He can get the glory. "God is our refuge and strength, a very present help in trouble." Psalm 46:1 "God is in the midst of her, she shall not be moved. God shall help her and that right early." Psalm 46:5 "Be still, and know that I am God. I will be exalted among the heathen, I will be exalted in the earth.

For the various things I experienced as a young teacher, a sheltered teacher, and a novice, I really needed the Lord and His encouraging words. Sunday School, Bible Study, and Testimony Service were key in my life and career. A teacher's classroom is compiled and combined of all kinds of students from all walks of life. We have to accept whatever comes through that door with our name on that schedule. My prayer to God was, "Lord you know how much I can take." God allows us to be in situations so that we can be stretched or get us out of our comfort zone. "There hath no temptation taken you but such as is common to man, but God is faithful, who will not suffer you to be tempted above that ye are able, but will with the temptation also make a way to escape, that ye may be able to bear it." 1 Corinthians 10:13

The three Hebrew boys were thrown in the fiery furnace bound together, but if God be for you, who can be against you? King Nebuchadnezzar was in shock to look inside the fiery furnace and see more than three men in there, he said, "Lo I see four men loose and the form of the fourth is like the Son of God." That is why I always thank God for cooling the flames. I know for a fact that God is concerned about our concerns. That is why the old adage says, what concerns you, concerns God as well. I personally thank God for being in all my business. He is very interested in my welfare and daily affairs. I love El Roi: "Thou God seest me." Genesis 16:13 You can go through anything, as long as you know, "The Big He, Seeth Me." That was key during my 35 years of teaching math and disciplining children, who were half-grown and experienced life like adults. You may have the age of a child or an adolescent, but your lifestyle is far from it. Several of my students had experienced things that I did not and will not ever encounter. God gave me the power and strength over the "giant's head" like he did David in the Bible. "So David prevailed over the Philistine with a sling and a stone, and smote the Philistine and slew him, but there was no sword in the hand of David." 1 Samuel 17:50

God gave me favor with my students, parents, and administration in the various schools I worked in, but ever now and then, Satan would try to work through one of my students, in terms of talking back and mouthing off. Most of the time, I did not have to write the students up. I had my own weapon and sword, and that was the Word of God. Sometimes God will put a Goliath in your life, for you to find the David within you. "Greater is he that is in you, than he that is in the world." I John 4:4. I would rebuke that devil in that student and that student immediately became subject. I would say, "Satan, the Lord rebukes you." The whole classroom would get quiet. "Satan, drop your weapon and flee." When you use this power, you better make sure you are walking with God wholeheartedly, because if not, you are out there on your own.

I remember the story in the Bible about the seven sons of Sceva. The seven sons of Sceva tried to use their power like Paul did, but Paul was a believer and God was with him, working miracles by Paul's hand. They talked to the evil spirits and said, "We adjure you by Jesus whom Paul preacheth." Acts 19:13b "And the evil spirit answered and said, Jesus I know, and Paul I know, but who are ye? And the man in whom the evil spirit was, leaped on them, and overcame them, and prevailed against them, so they fled out of that house naked and wounded." Acts 19:15-16. I knew that for the career I was in, I had to be prayed up, Worded up, and fasted up, to keep my sanity and stay in it for 35 years. I thank God that even though He is a Sovereign God, we can have a personal relationship, and we can talk to Him like a natural man. He knows our weaknesses, our uprising, and our downsitting. He knows how we feel. "Thou knowest my downsitting and mine uprising, thou understandest my thoughts afar off. Thou compassest my path and my lying down, and art acquainted with all my ways." Psalm 139:2-3 There were things that I had encountered and experienced that I could only share with God. We can always put our trust and confidence in God. "Neither is there any creature that is not manifest in his sight, but all things are naked and opened unto the eyes of him with whom we have to do." Hebrews 4:13

One good thing about my career, I had every summer off and holidays. I was able to attend prayer meetings with other teachers and get rejuvenated. I was revived, renewed, and refreshed every summer. It took that, and then some more, to have a peaceful school year. Do not tell me that God didn't work for me. He gave me joy in sorrow, hope for tomorrow, and a peace that passeth all understanding. He was my present help. He was my rock in a weary land. He increaseth my faith. He gave me holy boldness. He made my face like a flint. I never felt hopeless. He always kept my head lifted even when the chips were down. "But thou, O Lord art a shield for me, my glory and the lifter of mine head." Psalm 3:3 Sometimes my spirit was bowed down in humiliation, but my outward appearance, God covered me. "For the Lord will help me, therefore shall I not be confounded, therefore have I set my face like a flint and I know that I shall not be ashamed." Isaiah 50:7. I know God as a battle axe. "Thou art my battle axe and weapons of war: for with thee will I break in pieces the nations, and with thee will I destroy kingdoms; And with thee will I break in pieces the horse and his rider; and with thee will I break in pieces the chariot and his rider; With thee also will I break in pieces man and woman; and with thee will I break in pieces old and young; and with thee will I break in pieces the young man and the maid; I will also break in pieces with thee the shepherd and his flock; and with thee will I break in pieces the husbandman and his yoke of oxen; and with thee will I break in pieces captains and rulers." Jeremiah 51:20-23 When you walk with God, you never have to fight your own battles, God will fight for you. "For the weapons of our warfare are not carnal, but mighty through God to the pulling down of strongholds." 2 Corinthians 10:4 " Fear ye not, stand still, and see the salvation of the LORD, which he will shew to you to day: for the Egyptians whom ye have seen to day, ye shall see them again no more for ever." Exodus 14:13

I thank God for His son Jesus and for being our advocate, which means He can be your helper and intercessor, sitting on the right hand of the Father. He is a wonderful counselor. It is a wonderful thing when you can call God up. His line is never busy and He is never busy. God said He will answer before you call. I thank God that I have been taught to read God's Word daily. All of my answers and encouraging Words came directly from the Bible. Anyone who does not invest in Bible study and reading God's Word for themselves is doing a disservice. Satan knows the advantage, peace, and help one can get in reading the Bible daily. He keeps you busy on social media, playing games on the internet, watching TV, listening to the radio, or other carnal things which make the spiritual things of God very boring. You want to have a great relationship with God so that you will be able to stand against the wiles of Satan and recognize his tactics. "And the LORD said unto Satan, Whence comest thou? Then Satan answered the LORD, and said, From going to and fro in the earth, and from walking up and down in it." Job 1:7 "Because your adversary the devil, as a roaring lion, walketh about, seeking whom he may devour." 1 Peter 5:8b Temptations, tests, trials, and tribulations are going to come, but we must know and understand that we are overcomers, and God is a promise keeper. Always remember that God is the majority. So many times Satan will talk to you like he did to David. Satan told David there is no help for you from God. But David said, "But thou, O LORD, art a shield for me; my glory, and the lifter up of mine head. I cried unto the LORD with my voice, and he heard me out of his holy hill. Selah. I laid me down and slept; I awaked; for the LORD sustained me. Psalm 3:3-5

Chapter 7

I Was Bent, but Straightened by the Word

In my career, I also learned the power of praying and fasting. There are different kinds of fastings out there. Some people fast from watching TV, from the radio, being on Facebook, Instagram, and Twitter. Some fast from meats, desserts, soda pops, candy, shopping, or their favorite sitcoms. All of that is good, but the fast that I had chosen was to abstain from food and liquids from the time you wake up until 3:00 p.m. I have done this for over 40 years. It really works. I would do it faithfully, twice a year in August, because I had no inkling who my new students were or what kind of attitudes they would come with. And, I would fast in January, at the beginning of the school year. We would come back from a long winter and Christmas break. Children would have gotten into all kinds of devilment during the breaks, while their parents were at work. Statistics say more girls get pregnant at Christmas time than any other holiday. Christmas does bring about love, happiness, peace, joy, good times, happiness, and excitement. It can bring about future problems if used the wrong way, or not directed in the proper manner it is supposed to be. It should be about Christ and His birth, but so many people see it as the time he or she should be celebrated or adored. So these students come back with all kinds of spirits attached to them, from the freedom they were given by working parents and being latch-key children. Parents did not take the time to put things in place by taking a vacation at this time or sending them to their grandparents or other relatives. So, they would be left alone at home. Proverbs says, "The rod and reproof give wisdom: but a child left to himself bringeth his mother to shame." Proverbs 29:15

When the students returned from their long breaks, they would share what they had gotten into, those that did not, their friends became informants. Most of the time when boyfriends and girlfriends would break up, the girl would always come crying, looking for a shoulder to lean on, or someone to talk to outside of their parents. I would be the shoulder students felt comfortable leaning on to share their sad stories. This is the time when I could not just give my opinion or experiences. This is when I used the Word of God, which they could use from that day forward and even teach it to their children and friends. I also used that counseling as a witnessing tool, so I had to stay prayed and fasted up. "Howbeit this kind goeth not out but by prayer and fasting." Matthew 17:21 Sometimes the students would take heed, and others would do their own things; nevertheless, they had heard the truth and could just take it and put it on the shelf. As they matured and were encountered with the vicissitudes of life, they can always reach back and pull it off the shelf and say they remember their teacher telling them this or that while in school. They were too young to appreciate it then, but now that they are older and wiser, they can see clearly.

Fasting gives you power because the self is being crucified. Paul says, "I die daily." I Corinthians 15:31b The more you turn that plate down, your natural body is not as strong, then God can use you, and you are susceptible to hearing God. Self needs to be crucified so you may have an ear to hear, a heart to receive, and a mind to believe. "Create in me a clean heart, O God and renew a right spirit within me. Cast me not away from thy presence, and take not thy holy spirit from me." Psalm 51:10-11

The more I read the Word and meditated on the Word, it gave me stamina, tenacity, and authority to meet life's challenges head-on. No one knows or can predict the unexpectancies in our future. If God is the head of our lives and the center of our joy, we can endure hardness as a good soldier. If God be for you who can be against you? God's Word is everlasting. "For the Word of God is quick, and powerful, and sharper than any two-edged sword, piercing even to the dividing asunder of soul and spirit, and of the joints and marrow and is a discerner of the thoughts and intents of the heart." Hebrew 4:12 Remember, if you do not read God's Word daily, you are doing a disservice to yourself. God says to meditate on His Word day and night. We know that obedience is better than sacrifice. Obedience stands out as one of the premier qualities of biblical manhood. It requires faith to obey God when all the facts regarding a matter in your life may be unknown. Come what will or may, you will experience miraculous and glorious results. In my 35 years of teaching, God blessed me to master many things. I was the school's liaison, principal's administrative staff, student government advisor, majorette sponsor, senior class advisor, math chairman, school leadership board, extracurricular coordinator, trips sponsor, hospitality committee, program advisor, over teachers' activities, and community outreach.

Here I am as Senior Advisor on picture day.

God blessed me to implement these various activities, along with traveling out of town and attending math seminars from New Orleans to Boston, to Las Vegas, and then returning to Memphis and sharing what I'd learn. I wore many, many hats, but teaching math was my first priority and what I was licensed for. At the end of the day, I knew that was where my salary would come from. Teaching never became boring to me. I had so many other adventurous avenues that divided the monotony of teaching, grading papers, and recording grades. I had great, outstanding favor and blessings that I knew only God created for me. My career was laced with dichotomy, blessings, and testings. God knows how to bring balance to your life, to keep you humble and praying. During my career, I had to learn various cultures, the street word and the street world lingo, so I would be able to communicate with students.

There was a time when my car was an embarrassment. I would try to be the first one to pull off the parking lot because I would have to pat the accelerator seven times or more before it would crank up and I would be able to drive off. I was a well-dressed teacher but my car was a piece of work. There were a few mishaps; for example, a special needs student broke in my car the first year I started teaching and fractured my steering wheel with the alarm system. A student slid a sheet of paper under my classroom door at lunchtime calling me a female dog starting with the letter B. I would have to pick the paper up and ball it up before my next class, so it would not give them ideas. One of my students stole my bookends that held my books up but brought them back after I told him I was going to call the police; that was nobody but God.

I had invited two busloads of students from one of my former schools to come and participate in my Black History Program. They were of different nationalities and tongues. They dressed out in their native clothing and marched in on *"Coming to America,"* by Neil Diamond. It was a day one would never forget all the days of their lives to all that attended. All the nationalities were introduced to the Black culture. The Black culture was introduced to each of their cultures. Then we had a big lunch with all kinds of exotic foods. God was in it every step of the way. It was God that showed me how to orchestrate the day and program. Everybody was on a high plateau. The different kinds of clothes they had on from their country were absolutely amazing. Beautiful, bright, happy clothes that made a statement. The way they wore their hair and face made all up, showed me they invested a lot of time for that special event. Some of their music and dance was very interesting. Their appearance was so over the top and awesome. It was like a Miss America or Miss World Pageant. I closed the program out by saying, "Thank You and I Love You," in each one of their languages. I learned all seven languages the night before. That really went over well because no one was expecting it, and they knew someone had to teach me those different languages. Every time I spoke a different language, the applauding intensified. I felt so good and very elated that I could speak those various languages. If I messed up, no one knew but that certain nationality. They too, were happy that I tried to speak their language to a crowd of over 1500 people.

God always blessed me in everything I attempted to do. "And whatsoever he doeth shall prosper." Psalm 1:3b While the program was going on, someone broke into both buses, but my guests had brought their valuables inside the school and left their books. I was so embarrassed, but I thank God, the intruder was not able to get their personal goods. The principal of that school died the next year. I spoke about him previously in the book and how he was set to be honored and celebrated during the Black History Program before the unthinkable happened.

It was during the sixth year of my marriage when my husband left me. It was during the summer, while school was out and I was out of town. The burden of the household had fallen on me and my one income. Thank God we did not have any children. When school started back that August, I was broken, but God covered me with his feathers. "He shall cover thee with his wings shalt thou trust, his truth shall be thy shield and buckler." Psalm 91:4 I was so busy working with the senior class and planning their year's events, class day, class week, senior prom, senior picnic, senior trip, and senior t-shirts, I really had no personal time to drool and deal with what I was going through. The other times when I was not working on school activities, I was busy in my church, teaching Sunday School, singing in the choir, and doing odds and ends at the church. The only time my husband leaving me actually bothered me was maybe during the holidays and in the evenings when I would get home. I welcomed solitude, but not in the way it was given to me. I did make lemonade out of lemons. I would come home, read my mail, eat dinner, look at the news, prepare for the next day, pray, and go to sleep. I was alone, but I never felt lonely. God was my constant companion. God helped me up. He held me together. He covered me. God let me know, even though my husband left and I was hurting, embarrassed among family members and the ones who did know, that he was right there, telling me, "I Got You." "I am covering you." What you feel, I promise you others will not see. He let me know that He was "El Shadday," the all-sufficient God, eternally capable of being all that His people need. God reveals himself by how deeply He loves us and how effectively He cares for us. "For thy Maker is thine husband, the Lord of host is his name, and the Redeemer, the Holy One of Israel. The God of the whole earth, shall he be called. Isaiah 55:5

They had put a rumor out that I was married to an attorney who works long hours, but he really takes good care of me. How people came up with that, I do not know. It could have been because I wore very fancy clothes, high heels, a variety of wigs, fur coats, nice diamonds, drove a new Cadillac every three years, and did a lot of traveling. I found out with my walk with God, if you will be about your Father's business, He will be on top of your business, your well-being, your welfare, your spiritual growth, and practical living. "And he said unto them, How is it that ye sought me? wist ye not that I must be about my Father's business?" Luke 2:49

There were times in my suffering, testing times would seem greater than other times, but I will admonish everyone to read the 11th chapter of Hebrews in its entirety. You will get so much comfort out of that chapter, your faith will increase, and you will realize what you are going through is not worth speaking on and that it is just a light affliction. "For our light affliction which is but for a moment, worketh for us a far more exceeding and eternal weight of glory. While we look not at the things which are seen, but at the things which are not seen, for the things which are seen are temporal, but the things which are not seen are eternal." 2 Corinthians 4:17-18

Every test, trial, or tribulation we go through is for our good. It may not feel good, but it is for our good. It draws us closer to God. We have fellowship with Him more, we read the Word more, fast, and pray more. We even take notice of our conduct because we want to make sure we are walking circumspectly and our hands are clean. While we are going through, we don't want any hindrance to stand between us and God. We do not want our blessings to be put on hold or be aborted. When we read about the Heroes of Faith in the 11th chapter of Hebrews, we realize we can make it. You must believe and exercise four characteristics regarding faith and waiting on God's promises. First, you must come to grips that most victories are not overnight, some will be weeks, months, years, and some you may not live to see or witness. Secondly, you will be persuaded by the patriarchs in the Bible: Abraham, Isaac, and Jacob, their forefathers or the sons of Jacob. Thirdly, you must read God's Word and embrace it. Lastly, confess that you are a temporary resident on Earth who pleased God, not by your deeds, but rather by having great confidence in God. Walking with God is a faith walk, totally sold out to Him. Your eyes must be fastened on Him, knowing He is in control. He knows what is best for you. Nothing happens to you unless God allows it. Remember, whatever befalls us or betides us, we walk by faith and not by sight. "For ye have need of patience, that, after ye have done the will of God, ye might receive the promise." Hebrews 10:36

Being a saint, believer, or Christian, we must have a know-so salvation and not a hope–so salvation. "But if our gospel be hid, it is hid to them that are lost: In whom the god of this world hath blinded the minds of them which believe not, lest the light of the glorious gospel of Christ, who is the image of God, should shine unto them." 2 Corinthians 4:3-4 Once we realize that we are on the battlefield for our Lord and we are bought with a price, we are not our own, we know that God is sitting on the throne and putting things in place on our behalf for our good. "For the eyes of the Lord run to and fro throughout the whole earth, to shew himself strong in the behalf of them whose heart is perfect toward him?" 2

Chronicles 16:9 It means so much when God orders your steps and directs your path.

When I was in college, I did not know what to major in, but my father said, the world will always need doctors, teachers, and nurses. I knew then that was a true statement. I also knew that I had a weak stomach when it came to human flesh, needles, blood, bodily fluids, and sickness. The only thing that was left for me according to my father's suggestion was teaching. I could see myself standing in front of a body of students. I could see myself connecting with students and their parents because I have always been a people person. I have always been fond of teenagers and being "in the midst" than to have been around spoiled, crying babies, elementary kids, and junior high students. I knew that was not my niche. Although I was certified to teach K-12 and was also certified to be a principal and run a school, that was definitely not my calling.

Chapter 8

You Can't Have a One Night Stand with God

I majored in Business Administration with an emphasis in Education and Mathematics. My emphasis in mathematics was because I have always been extremely good at math. God blessed me to calculate math in my head without the aid of a pencil and paper or calculator. I took 9 weeks of student teaching, still a little indecisive, but my family members told me that if nothing else comes your way, you can always teach. I had 27 semester hours in math and needed three more in math for it to be a major. So, I started teaching math and was paid a regular teacher's salary because I had three years to go back and get my additional three hours. I worked at the school where, the college I attended was like three miles away, and my planning period at school was the same time as the math course I needed. Not only that, the professor who was teaching the math course was a friend of my friend. Therefore, he made allowances for me to be 10 minutes late coming from my job to his class. God was in the plan from the beginning to the ending. God is a strategist. He strategically put me in that particular school where I was needed so badly and with a principal that God gave me favor with.

Three years later after my retirement, the Board of Education called me and said there was an emergency. They asked if I would come and help push 90 seniors through mathematics for graduation. I would only have to work five hours a day and get $11,000. Well, you know that was $33 an hour. They did not take out anything because it was a grant. I had a choice of schools, so I went back to a school where everybody knew my name, and they were so happy that I came. I started the second week of February and ended the second week of May. I had all kinds of breaks, a whole week for Spring Break, Good Friday, a two-day Easter Break, Senior Skip Day, Senior Picnic Day, and seniors getting ready for prom that night break. It was worth my time, coming out of retirement. God gave me so much favor, and it was extraordinary. The students were very receptive toward me, and they would bring and buy my lunch. The parents were very nice as well. The colleagues were glad I came back. That is why, as I said before, it is very important to have a good name and reputation. The Board of Education said there was a great request for me. "A good name is rather to be chosen than great riches and loving favour rather than silver and gold." Proverbs 22:1 A good reputation is worth more than money.

Our God is a strategist. I was going to work every day, enjoying myself and getting the royal treatment. God sent me back to work because He knew what lied ahead of me. I had gone to work and bonded with my students for two and a half weeks. The following eight days, I received three phone calls from my siblings. They were not phone calls to see how I was doing after retirement. On February 25th, my sister was found dead in her sleep. Four days later, on March 1st, my mother died in her sleep. I received that information on the second phone call. I received the third call from my older brother that my husband had died in the hospital on March 3rd. I lost three loved ones in eight days, but God saw me through. I did not lose my mind. I did not faint. I did not scream down the hall, running out of the classroom. They asked me if I needed a ride home. I told them I appreciated the offer, but I was able to drive myself. God was with me. I was not upset with Him. I did not say, "Why me Lord?" or "God, you could have spread it out." It was just like He had prepared me for it. "But thou, when thou prayest, enter into thy closet, and when thou hast shut the door, pray to the Father which is in secret; and thy Father which seeth in secret shall reward thee openly." Matthew 6:6

My students were saying that if that had happened to them, they would have lost their minds and wouldn't have had the strength to walk or drive. They could not come back to work. Some even said, they would just die, too. People have always added this statement to the Bible, which is not in the Bible, "God will not put more on me than I can bear." In 2 Corinthians 1:8, Paul wrote, "For we would not, brethren, have you ignorant of our trouble which came to us in Asia, that we were pressed out of measure, above strength, insomuch that we despaired even of life." God allows hopelessness.

What we feel is hopeless without Him so He can appear in our lives and we can get closer to Him. After all your human resources have been depleted, if you know anything about a caring God, you can't help but run up in Him. "Surely he shall deliver thee from the snare of the fowler, and from the noisome pestilence. He shall cover thee with his feathers, and under his wings shalt thou trust: his truth shall be thy shield and buckler." Psalm 91:3-4 A snare of the fowler does not have to be people or a trap, it can be any uneasiness of the mind. God will rebuke it for our sake: loneliness, distress, unexpectancies, or disappointments.

God gave me victory over those giant's heads. There are truly benefits, blessings, joy, and peace in knowing the Lord for yourself. You can go to church every week, attend Sunday school weekly, and have Bible study to go along with all of that. But there is nothing like knowing God, one-on-one, through your tailor-made tests, trials, and tribulations, where you know all you have been through, and you did not lose your mind and received the victory in ways you know were impossible to win. But God was your stay, your vindicator, your "Abba Father", and your Savior. "They prevented me in the day of my calamity: but the LORD was my stay. He brought me forth also into a large place; he delivered me, because he delighted in me. The LORD rewarded me according to my righteousness; according to the cleanness of my hands hath he recompensed me. For I have kept the ways of the Lord and have not wickedly departed from my God." Psalm 18:18-21

At this particular time, my life was parallel with grief and trying to help seniors meet their graduation requirements in mathematics in 66 days. That is why I said earlier, God is a strategist. I did not have time to mope and sob over the loss of my loved ones because I had over 100 seniors who wanted to know if they would be able to graduate and if they would pass my class and receive their credit. Will they be able to march in May or will they have to go to summer school? My students were pulling on me and were excited about graduation. I did not have time to think about my personal life, my losses, and my shocks. I had to get excited with them and their big upcoming accomplishments, requirements, and commencement. Oh, I had the nicest principal in the world. He was so understanding and accommodating. He would always tell me he appreciated me coming out of retirement and helping with the seniors. He would tell me that, and it just really made me forget about my losses. He would see me daily and would say these words, and it seemed like they came from heaven, "I appreciate you, Doc." with a huge smile. It was very comforting at the time. Anyone who knows me, knows that I am very strong-willed, quick to laugh, smile a lot, and come across as outspoken, but believe it or not, I was kind-hearted and very soft on the inside. My personality is so strong, until sometimes people feel they have to use force with me, but it is the total opposite. They wind up raging, and I am totally quiet because they think that is what it takes to get their point across because my personality is so strong. Well, God made each one of us so different and unique. That is why I try to be nice and keep a spirit of giving about me. "I will praise thee, for I am fearfully and wonderfully made, marvelous are thy works, and that my soul knoweth right well." Psalm 139:14

My students had given me all kinds of sympathy cards along with my colleagues. I never got the chance to mourn because we had to clear things out concerning my mom, sell her home, and make provisions for her caregiver. Her caregiver, who was our childhood friend, lived with my mom and took care of her around the clock. We did our level best to set her up financially until she got on her feet. This was a big shock to her because she had to be uprooted after living with my mom for eleven years. She knew the day would come, but sometimes you never prepare for it until it happens. I guess one is living in denial until it happens. She had said she was going to live out of town with one of her cousins. I knew that was not the will of God for her life. God had better. He had given her a dream of where she would be living. She could not fathom the dream because the home the Lord had shown her was well over her head and income. When she came to live with me, she said that was the dream. Sometimes we try to interpret or understand dreams, but God has already put things in place for us without our help or understanding. That is the miracle He wrought for her.

As I am writing this book, she has been here for five years since my mom died. She has had great joy doing home care for people of means. She had great flexibility. She has been able to make a lot of money and be self-sufficient. She has gone beyond the call of duty concerning widows. The Lord has blessed her immensely. "Honor widows that are widows indeed." 1 Timothy 5:3 God has blessed her in the ministry to be blessed and be a blessing. Her children are blessed, and they are a great blessing to her as well. "And all thy children, shall be taught of the Lord, and great shall be the peace of thy children." Isaiah 54:13 "Lo children are an heritage of the Lord; and the fruit of the womb is his reward." Psalm 127:3 She has prayed for her two sons, and they have kept great jobs with prestige. Even when their company folded, they were still blessed to go to another company and still live very well. God has really encouraged her and blessed her. She has put in many hours in seeking God, crying out to Him, and lying out before the Lord. I have seen and heard firsthand. Her two sons are very supportive of me as well; they are my godsons. If they are not busy working long hours, they will do whatever you ask them to do. I have never had children but God has always put people in my life, to meet the needs of a daughter, son, or grandchildren. If you put God first and make Him the apple of your eye, the sky's the limit of what you can have, as the Clark sisters sing, "Just Believe and Receive It Today."

God has wrought so many miracles in my life. I want to encourage you through them. If He did it for me, He will do it for you because God has no respecter of person. The more the Lord does for me and blesses me, it truly increases my faith and trust in Him. God will pour you out a blessing that you will not have room enough to receive it. Even though we are experiencing a pandemic and people are not working, jobs have folded up for good, and everything in the city has not fully reopened. The Lord has blessed our cupboard and garage to be filled to capacity with the best meats that I have never purchased, name-brand groceries, organic foods, and foods only yuppies buy. Even though I have all these things and blessings, I have shared them with 12 families on my street and people at the church. God blesses us to be a blessing to others. God meets our basic needs and multiplies our seeds that we have sown into an abundance, so that we are able and should share with others. It also helps us to increase spirituality bearing the fruit of the spirit, love, joy, peace, and the other fruits flowing freely in our lives. When we experience this, we have no lack in God. "And God is able to make all grace abound toward you; that ye, always having all sufficiency in all things, may abound to every good work: As it is written, He hath dispersed abroad; he hath given to the poor: his righteousness remaineth for ever. Now he that ministereth seed to the sower both minister bread for your food, and multiply your seed sown, and increase the fruits of your righteousness." 2 Corinthians 9:8-10 God is my Jehovah Jireh, my provider. Jehovah Shalom, my peace. All His different names have been manifested in my life over and over again.

Testimonies

My mom was a writer, loved poetry, and was very poetic. My mom would always enter me into oratorical contests, and the Lord blessed me. I would always win first place for the most part. That helped me throughout high school, along with being in the drama club. It made it easier to speak in front of people. It even helped in my day-to-day affairs and handling business one-on-one. It instilled boldness and tenacity in me. Most of it stemmed from being in church. It is a great blessing, as well as a benefit, when parents raise their children in the church and in a positive environment at home.

My mom raised me in the fear of God at a very early age. We were taught to respect both parents. If my dad said no, no was the answer for both. If my mother said yes, yes was the answer for both. We could never say mama said I could when dad already said no. My dad would always say if he was in China, his answer would still be the same as my mom's. So we did not have to say, I am going to wait and ask dad. We were not able to play our parents against each other in making decisions toward us. That also taught us how to respect and honor both parents. "But continue thou in the things which thou hast learned and hast been assured of, knowing of whom you hast learned them; And that from a child thou hast known the holy scriptures, which are able to make thee wise unto salvation through faith which is in Christ Jesus." 2 Timothy 3:14-15

During my formative years, my parents taught us the Bible. My mom would have Bible study with us at any time, which we thought was always the wrong time. She was wise. We knew we were sheltered and different from the other children, but we did not have peer pressure, nor were we bullied. We just felt the way we were raised was normalcy. Although the other children had more freedom than us, they were able to wear short skirts and dresses. They went to games and sock hops. They could have little church boyfriends and girlfriends, and then it would extend even further than the church. It seems as if the children at our church blossomed so much quicker and faster than we did.

Our parents had a tight rope around us, but sometimes they would loosen it just a little to allow us to sing on the radio, sing around the city, and become a little more exposed to people who were different from us. So we were exposed to both worlds, but our parents taught us the fear of God and how to live saved. They taught us there is a heaven and a hell. That was always on the table of my heart. Even when we tried to have boyfriends, we really could not enjoy them at school because we already knew they wanted to call us on the home phone and wanted to come and visit you at home. My dad would always say, you can have as many male friends you want, but only one can come to the house and sit down. When I was old enough to date, I had several friends that I would go out with, but they were not allowed to come in and sit down. My dad said he did not want them to fight or argue over me. He told us about a man on his job whose daughter had two different guys coming over, and one started shooting. That was all my dad needed to hear. He would always remind me of that. He told me that was not going to happen in our home. We could not get wild in the world because my mother would always say, "What if you died tonight and you are not saved?" God already knew I was His. He knew that I was going to be saved at an early age. I could not sin in peace. I had a calling on my life. "Preach the word, be instant in season, out of season, reprove, rebuke, exhort with all longsuffering and doctrine." 2 Timothy 4:12

Our parents brought us up on drugs. We were drug to Sunday School. We were drug to Bible study. We were drug to midweek services. We were drug to revivals. Whatever service they had at church, our parents drug us there. A lot of times, the pastor's children would not even be there, but we were drug there. As children, we resented all of that, and if you thought that was a lot, we were taken to prayer meetings before we started 1st grade and throughout high school. We did not know the effect that would have on our lives.

After I graduated from college and started teaching a hard subject like math to high school students, I needed every prayer I could get. During my summers off from school, I started going to prayer meetings the entire summer. If I went out of town, I would get right back in prayer meetings as soon as I returned from my vacation.

Back then, we would start back to work right after Labor Day, but now, they go back in early August. I could tell I had been with God that summer and He was first priority. My students would behave, get to class on time, and have their books and materials. They would say, "yes and no ma'am," to me, and I was in my early twenties. The same students would go down the hall and sit in their other classes and would be disrespectful, late for class, with no materials, talkback, and the like. My colleagues would pass by and say, he or she acts differently in your room. They couldn't believe it was the same student. But I used the prayer recipe, praying in the summertime at the prayer meetings and praying in my secret closet at home before coming to school. I would put blessed oil over the doorpost, on the pencil sharpener, their desks, and around the trash can area. Students loved to get up and throw away paper, for whatever reason. Whatever it was, the oil was in the atmosphere.

Readers, it worked then and it worked for 35 years. I could have retired before I did, but I stayed for 35 years because of the joy my students brought me and the peace I had daily with high school students, even though sometimes, I would have a few challenges.

God does not want us to get relaxed and complacent in Him. "Woe to them that are at ease in Zion." Amos 6:1a Sometimes in life, we feel we have everything all sewn up and in check. Then we get slack in our prayer life and get slack in seeking Him. God knows exactly how to get our attention and keep us on our toes. We have been taught that when we are going through a difficult situation, not to ask the Lord to get us out of the test, but what does He want us to get from the test. In other words, "Lord, what are you saying?" "In everything give thanks for this is the will of God in Christ Jesus concerning you." 1 Thessalonians 5:18

***

My sister worked in the school system just as I did. She was not as attentive to the prayer meetings as I was in the summer. I am telling you when school would reopen, she would have so many problems, issues, and always complaining about the things on her job. They were very minute to us. But to her, it was like a mountain. Many of the situations did not involve her, but Satan took her peace because he knew her prayer life was not up to par. "The horse is prepared against the day of battle, but safety is of the Lord." Proverbs 21:31 The success of your battles, tests, issues, or whatever your circumstances, depends on your prayer life. Satan lives to attack the mind. He wages his attacks on the mind because with our minds we serve the Lord. He wants to keep us focused on uncertainties and problems we cannot solve, so we will not have peace. "Thou will keep him perfect peace, whose mind is stayed on thee, because he trusteth in thee." Isaiah 26:3

I do know, from a young teacher to a retired 35-year teacher, the more quality time you give God in prayer, the more quality time God will give you in peace. My whole life is centered around prayer. If there were ever a time we should make Jesus the head of our lives and the center of our joy, the time is now. We are living in a very dark world and a very dark time. We are experiencing things that man has never experienced before. My mom would say it was a time that man has never seen and God has seldom seen. In the blink of an eye, the whole world has changed. Everywhere you go or look, everybody is wearing a mask due to the coronavirus outbreak, whether it is comfortable or not. "This know also, that in the last days perilous times, shall come." 2 Timothy 3:1 "All these are the beginning of sorrows." Matthew 24:8

God speaks in so many different ways. Some can hear and take heed and others say, it's just life. Some will fear, and when I say fear, I do not mean frightfully, I mean in a reverent way. "The fear of the Lord is the beginning of wisdom and the knowledge of the holy is understanding." Proverbs 9:10 When you reverence God and have a relationship with Him, it is coupled with trust and most importantly, love, because God is Love. God has shown love toward us immensely in so many facets, but the true love we know is when He gave His only begotten Son. God gave us His best, and He wants our best, and that is our soul. He wants it all TODAY. "While it is said, Today if ye will hear his voice, harden not your hearts, as in the provocation." Hebrews 3:15

***

God has always looked out for me and covered me, even when I was not walking with Him nor living for Him. I remember when I was student teaching at 21, I went back to the high school I graduated from. I was very comfortable there with the principal, administration, and faculty. God has always bestowed favor upon me. I had chosen to be under the typing teacher I had when I was going there. This was only three years later. When I was her student, she would always give me good conduct grades, even though I was playful and a little talkative. The other students noticed as well because their conduct grades were not good. So I chose her to do my student teaching under, but I noticed her personality had changed towards me since three years ago. I tried to endure and overlook it because it was only going to be for nine weeks. I was not happy. I complained to my principal and my professor. My principal explained to me what was going on. He said she felt threatened and insecure, thinking maybe I would come back and take her job because business administration was my major as well. That was nowhere on my mind to come back to that school at all for a teaching position. I wanted to go somewhere different with all new administration and staff. I was the one that was insecure and unsure, but nevertheless, I was moved to a math teacher that I did not have when I was going there. I was so happy with her, and she made me feel welcomed. She gave me great pointers for becoming a new teacher. She was everything I needed. I enjoyed being under her tutelage and auspice. She gave me good grades and a great evaluation.

My graduation date came fast because I was really enjoying her. I graduated from college that spring with a BS Degree in April. I gave my life to God nine months later. I gave up everything to follow God wholeheartedly. I had a choice to make. "Choose you this day, whom ye will serve, but as for me and my house, we will serve the Lord." Joshua 24:15b,15d

I will not write that it was easy because it was a culture change for me. I was changing from the worldly culture to the kingdom culture. I had to go back to school again. This school was very different than the mundane. I had and have a Master Teacher...God. You do not ever graduate, but grow in grace. "But grow in grace, and in the knowledge of our Lord and Saviour Jesus Christ. To Him be glory both now and for ever. Amen 2 Peter 3:18

You take and live one day at a time. Live each day like it is your last day because you never know when it is your last time to repent and come to the Lord. Just like regular school, you are going to fail, but God will be right there to pick you up when you fall. God is a gentleman. If you want to lie there and wobble, He will stretch His hands to you, but you will have to take His Hand. You will have to have a made-up mind to walk the straight and narrow path. The kingdom culture, which I mentioned earlier, is not a system of rules, but a new concept of life. "Enter ye in at the straight gate: for wide is the gate, and broad is the way, which leadeth to destruction, and many there be which go in thereat: Because strait is the gate, and narrow is the way, which leadeth unto life, and few there be that find it." Matthew 7:13-14

In this particular school, you do not take breaks or holidays. If you decide to do that, you will be well off course. You will be giving place to the enemy. You study daily, you take notes, you run references, you collect, and you gather other biblical books that are related. You do not take off on the weekends; you stay the course. This is a 24 hours/7 days a week course. Even though you do well, you are not exempted from tests. In the kingdom culture, your tests come to make you stronger. "And thou shalt remember that the Lord your God led you all the way these forty years in the wilderness, to humble you, and test you, to know what was in your heart, whether you would keep His commandments or not." Deuteronomy 8:2 "Examine me, O' Lord, and prove me, try my mind and my heart." Psalm 26:2 In this particular school, the teacher is always available. He never sleeps nor slumber. He is an on-time God and he will answer you before you call. "Behold, he that keepeth Israel shall neither slumber nor sleep." Psalm 121:4 "And it shall come to pass, that before they call, I will answer and while they are yet speaking, I will hear." Isaiah 65:24 With this Master Teacher, you do not get grades, but you do get rewards. "But without faith, it is impossible to please him: for he that cometh to God must believe that he is, and that he is a rewarder of them that diligently seek him" Hebrews 11:6

God's pay is out of this world. After we die, that is when we will stand before Him in judgement; death is not our end. Some people say, "When you are dead, you are done." Death is not the end, it is your destiny's door. "And as it is appointed unto men once to die, but after this the judgement." Hebrew 9:27 We all are going to have eternal life, but the choice is who are you preparing to spend it with: God or Satan? "Therefore hell hath enlarged herself and opened her mouth without measure." Isaiah 5:14a This Master Teacher, teaches you and then hires you to become His ambassador and living epistle. "And said unto them. Go ye, also in the vineyard, and whatsoever is right I will give you." Matthew 20:4 "Ye are our epistle written in our hearts, known and read of all men." 2 Corinthians 3:2a

***

When my husband left me, that is when I enrolled in God's school full-time. In this life, you will experience a lot of unpleasantries and unexpectancies. God will take care of you and assign you your own personal ministering angels to be with you in your dark hours and wilderness experiences. Even when you are down in the valley, you are not going to stay because David says, "Yea though I walk through the valley of the shadow of death, I will fear no evil, for thou art with me, thy rod and thy staff they comfort me." Psalm 23:4 "He maketh me to lie down in green pastures, he leadeth me beside the still waters." Psalm 23:2 Even though God has blessed me to obtain four degrees including my doctorate, and have retired from working after three and a half decades, I am still in school today. The school I am in now, you do not retire or graduate from. Only death brings you to the end. That is what I am striving for, to be absent from the body and to be in the presence of the Lord. This accomplishment I am working on and striving for is out of this world. You have to be totally sold out to God and you must come through his Son Jesus. The Bible says if you come any other way you come as a thief. "Jesus said unto him, I am the way, the truth, and the life: no man cometh unto the Father, but by me." John 14:6

I have heaven in my view. This Earth is my preparation room. This world is not my home. I am just a pilgrim on my way home. I did not come to stay here. I tremendously love the BIBLE because everybody needs this to get to heaven. It is the Basic Instruction Before Leaving Earth. That is why you have to have it. I had some very dark days and some lonely nights when my husband left. I had to stand still and see the salvation of the Lord. I did not go to the left nor the right. Many days, I was waiting on God to speak and tell me what to do, or which direction to go. At that time, God did not open His mouth, but I knew He was with me because I had peace and contentment in the fire. I had nowhere to go and no one to turn to but God. When you are in a test, the Bible says to study to be quiet. "In quietness and in confidence shall be your strength and ye would not." Isaiah 30:15 It means you refused to be quiet about your situation. Your everyday conversation is what you're going through. People hate to speak to you and ask you how you are doing. You are going to spend over half an hour telling them your problems. You weigh people down with your tests. No battle is ours, it belongs to the Lord. "And he said, Hearken ye, all Judah, and ye inhabitants of Jerusalem, and thou king Jehosophat, Thus saith the Lord unto you, Be not afraid nor dismayed by reason of this great multitude; for the battle is not yours, but God's." 2 Chronicles 20:15 We are to stay sweet and humble, so people will be able to tell the difference between holy and unholy. "Let your light so shine before men that they may see your good works, and glorify your Father which is in heaven." Matthew 5:16

I took those wedding vows, April 23, 1988. I took it seriously, come what may. I never believed in divorce or marrying man after man. It had nothing to do with my spiritual beliefs or convictions. That was plain ole Aretha's make-up. I just believe one man on this big Earth is enough, unless God has a purpose for us, and not our flesh. If we were living to satisfy our flesh, we would have multiple mates and many, many spouses, just to please the lust of the eyes, the lust of the flesh, and the pride of life. My mom would always say, "Burying one man is enough in a lifetime." For years, I thought my husband would come back. So many people prophesied to me and said, "He'll be back." I assumed they were talking about my husband, and they assumed when they were prophesying, they were talking about my husband. But the Bible says, "For we know in part and we prophesy in part." I Corinthians 13:9 He did not come back, plus he got sick and died young. I asked God what did it mean when different prophets, whom I know you use mightily, told me, "He will be back." They never told me who "He" was. "All things are lawful for me, but all things are not expedient, all things are lawful for me, but all things edify not." 1 Corinthians 10:23

But as the old saying goes, you will understand it by and by. But God is good. I was able to stay focused on my husband and not get sidetracked by other men who were trying to make their appeal. After so many years, he hadn't come back but God still blessed me financially. So it really did not matter to me, if he came home or not. God has smiled on me and really made me glad. God gave me beauty for every one of my ashes.

***

I remember when I entered college back in the '70s, the counselor asked me if I'd taken the ACT. I said no and thought nothing of it. So she told me I would have to take the test before I entered college. I took it. I thought it was like any other exam. I did not know it was a great mandated test. I took the test but did not take it seriously. On my college transcript, there will always be a score of 14, and it is a constant reminder that I did not take it seriously. Nevertheless, I was accepted into college that summer, but I had to take remedial courses in English and Math. God blessed me to do extremely well. When school started that fall, I advanced in math rapidly than my peers and became a tutor for statistics. I did not know it then because I was in darkness, but when I look back now, I can see clearly. He was there all the time. My college days were so much fun and rewarding. I was living with my parents. I had some guidelines and house rules that I had to abide by. My parents still respected me and treated me like an adult. I thank God for how my parents raised me, but back then, I did not appreciate it. It taught me discipline, even when I became grown and in the workplace.

I noticed so many of my colleagues had problems on the job in respecting leadership because they were not raised with the firmness I had as a child. I have always had it easy in respecting leadership and authority because my parents reared us that way. The average child would be slow and stubborn in moving when the parents would speak to them. We had to move instantly or felt the belt instantly. We had a choice, so we chose the first one. Because of the way I was brought up, I can endure a lot of things spiritually and naturally. I have learned over the years from teaching that parents who have not raised their children properly are doing a disservice to their children and themselves. For the most part, as parents began to age, their children did not have the love, honor, and respect for them. Therefore, they did not feel obligated to help in assisting with their parents in their latter days to pick up the phone and call them, drop by weekly to help with chores, or just sit down and spend some quality time, which shows you care.

My parents knew they could depend on me for their chores, picking up food, carrying them out to eat, and getting whatever they wanted for birthdays, Mother's Day, Father's Day, and Christmas. I knew I would be in their shoes one day, a senior citizen and elderly. I did not have children of my own. "Cast thy bread upon the waters, for thou shalt find it after many days." Ecclesiastes 11:1

Doing good deeds without looking for anything in return will always give you great dividends, unforeseen. I am in my mid-sixties, without any children, but God, who is Jehovah Jireh, provided me with three friend girls, who I can depend on, four godsons, two goddaughters, and one in the making, who was born just eight years ago. I have a host of friends and associates who are very generous toward me. I cannot leave out my nieces and great-nieces. My siblings are also there for me. So far, I do not need them at this time. But, I thank God I know the door is always opened. "A man that hath friends must shew himself friendly, and there is a friend that sticketh closer than a brother." Proverbs 18:24

Always practice being nice, patient, tolerant, kind, and sensitive. Although people might not pay you back with the same attitude, God said, "Whatsoever is right, I will give you." Matthew 20:4b God does the reciprocation, not man. Whatever needs I have in my life, God surely provides for me, and that is why I live for Him and I do not want to do anything to disappoint God. Many times I have stumbled, but God knew my heart. He was right there to pick me back up. That is what I know and love about God. God told me by one of the mothers in the church, that I was His darling. Ever so often, I encourage myself with that statement. "Darling" in the Bible means dearly beloved, favorite, regarded with great kindness and tenderness. Hallelujah. Hallelujah.

***

I left my parent's home at the age of 31. That was the age I got married. I enjoyed living with my parents while I was there, but I was ready to be on my own. I left in good standing, which says a lot in times like these. My husband and I lived downtown, so I had great access to them and the church, which was a blessing and the plan of God. I was very enthralled to have a successful marriage under the umbrella of holiness. My marriage was calm, quiet, and unified. My husband was very domesticated and husband-oriented. He would make the bed, wash the clothes, and come to my job every Friday to take my car to get it professionally cleaned. He would also leave me a generous allowance on his payday which was every other Friday. He never asked me what I made or what I was doing with my money. He was such a gentleman, non-confrontational, considerate of others, and always giving. But he was a "Mama's Boy" which posed problems sometimes. His mom did not particularly care for me. We were two women in love with the same man. Her only son and my husband. She was very sarcastic. Being young and not used to that kind of behavior, I joined in the sarcasm. I did not know anything else to do. My husband would always tell her to be nice and civil. She wanted me to know that I was not her cup of tea, nor her bread and butter. When she would speak, she would immediately say, let me speak to my son. I endured. I did not tell my mother or father how she treated me. As a matter of fact, I did not share it with anyone, outside of my husband. He was not the kind of son that would go toe-to-toe with his mother or sit down and talk about the issue with her. He knew she was wrong, but being threatened by me overrode self-discipline. I had heard about in-law issues, but I never thought that would ever knock at my door. The scripture is right, "Be sober, be vigilant, because your adversary the devil, as a roaring lion, walketh about, seeketh whom he may devour." 1 Peter 5:8

My husband left me after six years of marriage, and I never saw it coming. After he left, I always felt he would come back because I thought we had stability and soundness in our marriage and we pretty much came from similar backgrounds. So, I kept the faith that he would be back. I waited on my husband for weeks. Weeks turned into months. Months turned into years. Years were turning into decades. We were separated longer than we were together. Well, my husband passed at an early age and did not come back as the prophets and prophetesses told me. As I said before, God brought it to my attention that they never told me that the "He" they were prophesying about was my husband. God told me who the "He" was, but it is too premature to talk about or discuss or let alone reveal a name. I have much comfort in the prophecy, even though we know prophecies come in part.

God never makes a mistake. Everything we go through should be a teachable moment, and also where we ask God, "What do you want me to get out of this?" rather than, "Lord, when will I get out of this?" Right about now, I am very happy and content. I want to continue to focus and keep my mind on God, so I can absorb that perfect peace.

My parents always told my siblings and me not to be so quick to get a divorce because you never know what is going to happen to your mate and you will receive his or her benefits. Well, we stayed separated and we never got a divorce. When he passed, I called the social security office to see what was what. I called just at the right time. He was already receiving a social security disability check, so I was able to get all of that. I had no idea or inkling he was receiving a check of a little over $2200 monthly. He passed on the third of March. His check was mailed out two days later, and his father sent it back in err on the side of caution. The social security office told me to bring two documents: our marriage license and death certificate. My siblings and one of my nieces, who grew up in the home with me, kept telling me that my husband had gotten married again. One of my quiet siblings called from out of town and said that she heard my husband had gotten married again. Four of my siblings would repeat this in my ear periodically. But after the quiet sibling mentioned it to me, I began to wonder. Maybe it is true, even though we never got a divorce. Although some men do polygamy, I never thought he would. But you cannot put anything past anyone these days and times. So I went downtown to the marriage license bureau to see what's what because your social security number follows you all over the United States. I was curious to know if he'd gone to another state and gotten married. The lady took the social security number and told me he was only married to me, and she gave me a copy of our marriage license, which was needed for me to get all his benefits. His father left my name off of the obituary and said I was unknown. When part of the death certificate asked the name of the current and previous wife, the father put my name as unknown. If God is for you, who can be against you? I had to pay $35 for a copy of my own husband's death certificate because my father-in-law said I was unknown. I paid the $35 for the death certificate and took it along with my marriage license to the social security office. When that lady finished reading out to me what I was going to get monthly, I was like in a trance. I immediately remembered what my parents told me, "Do not be so quick to divorce." I also honored my wedding vows I made and recited before God. When my husband first left me, I wanted him so badly after a few years down the road. The Lord had blessed me. It did not matter if I never saw him again because I had outgrown him. For the sake of the vows and obeying God, I was going to endure it. God knew that and my heart. God just took him, so that I could be free, through death, not a common divorce. If you have a relationship with God and a daily prayer life, God will work for the one who is praying consistently and daily. I am a living testimony. Prayer works. If my husband had come back, I would have been a winner. And when God saw fit to call him in, I was still a winner in the army of the Lord.

The social security lady told me as his widow, I would receive his $2300 monthly, his last check his father sent back for March 2016, and also the $2055 from social security for death and burial. I received all that then and still am receiving it now. When I first moved into my home without him, I struggled to pay the mortgage and utilities. His monthly check pays my mortgage and utilities. With God, you will never lose. There will be times when you feel all alone and you feel defeated. That is why it is important to know the scripture, so you can be encouraged during the dark times. That's why we do not have to doubt God in darkness, what He told us in the light. We have to be just like David. Encourage ourselves and wait on God. Our patience possesses our souls. Waiting time is not wasted time with God. The devil will magnify the waiting time because that is his job. Our job is to look at how big our God is and not how big the problem is.

I thank God that when my husband left me, it was at a time when I was truly and thoroughly involved in my job. Teaching math is very critical and crucial. I was the head over so many departments and the liaison for the school. So I did not have time to wiggle my fingers and rub my hands together, wondering what I was going to do and crying, "Woe is me." My job was very demanding in a positive way. When I went home I was glad for the "me time." I could relax without anyone depending on me for anything. I would fall asleep, and the next day would come, and I would get up, pray, read the Bible, and prepare for work. I learned that your emotions are driven by your pattern. They say you are what you eat. You are what you think. If you think you are lonely and insecure, then you will feel lonely and insecure. "In quietness and in confidence shall be your strength." Isaiah 30:15b This scripture is very encouraging when you are waiting on God to fix a situation or to help you receive victory in a battle. "But they that wait upon the Lord shall renew their strength, they shall mount up with wings like eagles, they shall run, and not be weary, and they shall walk, and not faint." Isaiah 40:31

During the test, God took care of me like an eagle takes care of her young. God would definitely cover me with his feathers. I could feel the strength of God as I was going through the thorns and the thistles. God's grace was undeniably sufficient for me. Oftentimes, people will tell you, "I know God," but does God know you? We all know the president, by name and by face, but does he know us? If you truly know Him, you will know he's an on-time God. When you are facing a test, I will tell the world the outlook looks gloomy, but the uplook is Glorious. There is something mighty sweet about the Lord. Eyes have not seen it, ears haven't heard it, the great things God has in store for His people. Our God is an awesome God.

He reigns forever and forever.

God gave me much beauty for my ashes. I told the Lord, "I could be so much further in life if my husband was here because I knew two incomes were better than one." God spoke to me with a very strong, fervent voice and said, "I am Time." In other words, God was letting me know He makes up for time. "I will restore to you the years that the locust hath eaten, the cankerworm, and the caterpillar, and the palmerworm, my great army which I sent among you. And ye shall eat in plenty and be satisfied, and praise the name of the Lord your God, that hath dealt wondrously with you, and my people shall ever be ashamed." Joel 12:25-26 God said in Isaiah 54:5, He is our maker and our husband. "The grass withers and the flowers fade, but the word of our God stands forever." Isaiah 40:8

God knew where to put me. My husband and I lived in a condo on the river that housed the city mayor, congressman, Isaac Hayes, other entertainers, attorneys, city officials, two news anchors, pastors, bishops, teachers, and other counselors. It was a very prestigious place. I helped my goddaughter move there and my brother and sister. It was the place to be. We had 24-hour maintenance, security, grocery store, swimming pool, spa, work-out room, and they sponsored a party every holiday. I was alone, but not lonely. You would always run into someone on the elevator or in the mailroom or getting out of your car. I thank God for placing me there, because God knew my future, because I did not. We always want God to order our steps. "The steps of a good man are ordered by the Lord and he delighteth in his way." Psalm 37:23

God took me up in my finances, in purchasing vehicles,

traveling, getting my doctorate degree, being called to the ministry, getting ordained, and speaking on the Word Network. God has given me excellent godsons and goddaughters. I never wanted any babies or young children. I wanted my children to be born a teenager at 17 years and older, which is impossible. I did not know I would have any godchildren whatsoever. They have been there for me because they are of God. God knows what I need and what I want.

I lived downtown so most of the schools I taught in were either in downtown and midtown. My church was ten minutes away. Everything was sort of at my fingertips. When you are going through, God knows how to lighten the load and cool the flames. I was also three minutes away from our Holy Convocation. As I stated earlier, I was ten minutes away from my parents. I appreciate God and how He strategically sets up things. I lived there on the river, in that big condo that God blessed me with for 12 years, without anyone's assistance. God did it. If anything would break, it would be fixed in 24 hours. I did not have to deal with landscaping or lawn services, no utilities, and no association fees. I was given two free parking spots because I had been there for a while. That was God. God gave me constant reminders that He was with me and was working for me, in the midst of all I was going through. His eyes were fixed on me. I could literally feel God holding me tight.

I was at the beauty shop and the hairstylist asked another client where she had been, and she said her husband left her six months ago. This was during the same time my husband left me. She said she has not combed her hair or her daughter's hair in six months.

God let me hear that, although I was under the dryer. He wanted me to see that I could have had that same experience. I was grateful to witness that and to know that God had me and was holding me up with His right hand and holy arms. So many times you think your situation or test is horrible until you hear what the next person is going through. Then you realize your test is a piece of cake compared to others. I remember one of my siblings said that if you would put 10 people in a circle, give them a sheet of paper, tell them to write down what they are going through, leave it nameless, fold it up, and have them drop it in a bag. Then, someone would read the folded papers, and you would realize that others are worse off than you. Everybody's test is tailored made for them. God will never put any more on you than you can bear.

***

I was a substitute teacher before I became a regular teacher. Therefore, I would sub in various schools, in various areas, with children being from different walks of life. God had my career designed that way to broaden my horizons and work with various cultures, social-economical levels, and religions. Since I had come up in a sheltered environment, I needed to become involved with students that were different than me. That helped me tremendously, and I was able to teach at any school and work comfortably with all kinds of principals, teachers, and school staff. People I had questions about, did not raise my eyebrow, neither did they make me feel insecure. The students that were different from me were the ones I enjoyed the most, and they gravitated towards me. Opposites really do attract. Those students made me stronger and increased my stamina and tenacity. Sometimes when students would be too challenging, I knew I had to increase my prayer time. That is when the normalcy would occur. It never was about my students; it was God making me and getting me ready for ministry. Your tests come to make you better, not bitter. Whenever my students' behavior was noticeable or I had unexpected challenges, I knew what time it was. It was time for me to upgrade my spiritual works, praying more, fasting more, and reading God's Word.

When I would do these things, everything would go back to normalcy. I thank God that He gets our attention that way, so we can come up in our spiritual works for Him. Not only are we to be hearers, but we have to be doers as well. "But be ye doers of the word, and not hearers only, deceiving your own selves. For if any be a hearer of the word, and not a doer, he is like unto a man beholding his natural face in a glass: For he beholdeth himself, and goeth his way, and straightway forgetteth what manner of man he was. But he who looks into the perfect Law of Liberty and continues in it, and is not a forgetful hearer but a doer of the work this one will be blessed in what he does." James 1:22-25 I thank God for this great revelation during the 35 years of teaching, even in everyday practical living. Flesh and blood cannot reveal this, only El Roi, thou God seest me. It means so much to have a one-on-one relationship with God daily, not just when you are in trouble. God does not want us to call Him only when we are in trouble. He wants a day-to-day personal relationship when things are going well with you. That proves to Him, you are honoring and worshipping Him. It is like a person in love with a mate. He or she wants to hear from them two and three times a day, or maybe throughout the day and night. That is how God wants to hear from us. He wants to be first priority, first place on our minds, and first in our lives. Otherwise, this is the message for you: "I also will laugh at your calamity; I will mock when your fear cometh; When your fear cometh as desolation, and your destruction cometh as a whirlwind; when distress and anguish cometh upon you. Then shall they call upon me, but I will not answer; they shall seek me early, but they shall not find me." Proverbs 1:26-28

I thank God for my two best friends. We left high school together, started college together, even took remedial courses together leading up to our freshmen year in college. My friends always looked up to me to ask questions, ask for things, get things, and strive for excellence. We always worked out well together. Drilled each other. And I must admit, we made little tiny cheat sheets, just in case we could not remember everything. All of our professors loved us, noticed us, we had favor with them, and they admired the unity we had. Post-education becomes so much easier when you have close partners or friends to share your goals, dreams, and good grades with. We joined a sorority and ran for various titles of the school. As I said earlier, I won the title of Miss Senior. And when you open up our annual yearbook, the first picture you see is me standing by that Rolls Royce with a Show dog.

Sometimes God will show people your future, and it is not good all the time. Sometimes He will show people the negatives in your life, presently, or what is coming up the road. That is for that person to start interceding for you in prayer and asking God to turn the evil away. That is why we must intercede and pray for one another, whether we have a personal relationship or not.

I always carried myself like a church lady, not on purpose, it was embedded in me from a child up. You better believe, back then, I wanted to look like the other cool girls and not a church girl. Little did I know, it was to my advantage, even though I thought it was unpopular. That was and is the virtue God has blessed me with through my entire life by being different, dressing differently, and wearing pearls with everything, which accents my pearly white teeth. My dentist always says that I have "toilet white teeth."

When I graduated from college, I had all my credentials and was ready to be a math teacher. I did not receive my call right away like my other classmates. So I just kept working at City Hall and had a glorious time. I worked there from Spring, right after graduation until November. I received a call from a principal to be a long-term substitute teacher for the entire year. I was happy and so glad to start teaching. But boy was I green, inexperienced, and uninformed, but so quickly, I matured. I became sober and stepped up to the plate. The students knew I was a young new teacher, but they also knew there was something different about me in terms of my character and the way I dressed. Because of these two factors, the students respected me. Colleagues and principals would always remark on how I was a very strong disciplinarian, being so young. It was God, prayer, fasting, and blessed oil. Those were the tools that took me through my whole 35 years. There are times in my life that no one had to tell me to draw close to God. Tests, trials, and tribulations would always run me up in God. "Draw nigh to God and he will draw nigh to you." James 4:8 God had me in the palm of His hand. Literally. God knew the things to make me come running to Him.

Dr. Aretha Coleman-Terry

Chapter 9

The Good Kept Me Knowing God, The Bad Kept Me Searching for God

My job, my career, and my livelihood, always kept me on my knees. I thank God for the motivation He instilled in my personal life to keep me praying and seeking Him. Everything we go through in life is tailor-made for us. There are no mistakes or mishaps in our lives. God knows who we are and all the things we will encounter, the good, the bad, and the ugly, before the foundation of the world. The Good kept me knowing God. The Bad kept me looking to God. The Ugly kept me closer to God. Through it all, I have learned to trust in Jesus. I have learned to depend on Him. I understand very well when David said, "It is good for me that I have been afflicted, that I might learn thy statutes." Psalm 119:71

All of our experiences in life should be surrounded by the

natural and the spiritual realm. When our encounters are not positive, we should not ask, "Lord, when will I get out of this, but Lord, what can I learn from this?" God has a set time, a victory date, a deliverance date, and an overcomer date. The only thing we have to do is stay the course, do not throw in the towel, and realize that waiting time is not wasting time with God. We are more than conquerors. "Nay, in all these things we are more than conquerors through him that loved us." Romans 8:37

Paul asked a question, which should always be soul-shaking and life-threatening. The following verse should cause us to take inventory of our life and our life should be measured by it daily. "Who shall separate us from the love of Christ? Shall tribulation, or distress, or persecution, or famine, or nakedness, or peril, or sword? As it is written, For thy sake we are killed all the day long; we are accounted as sheep for the slaughter. For I am persuaded, that neither death, nor life, nor angels, nor principalities, nor powers, nor things present, nor things to come, Nor height, nor depth, nor any other creature, shall be able to separate us from the love of God, which is in Christ Jesus our LORD." Romans 8:35-36, 38-39

Whenever God allows us to go through something, it is for many reasons, but most of all, it is to humble us, and prove us, and know what is in our hearts. Only God knows the heart. We think we know ourselves and others do, but God is the only one who knows the heart of every man. We look at the outward appearance. We go by what we see and what we feel about the individual. That is why women and men marry spouses that will be the death of them because he or she feels they know the heart of that individual. However, the outward appearance, which is so alluring, can be confused with the individual's heart. We would not have so many divorces, homicides, or suicides if we really knew the heart of that individual.

When my husband left me, I had just purchased a fully-loaded vehicle that CEOs drive. After he left, I had to continue to lease our townhome, pay the phone bill, insurance, etc. Everything was left on my school teacher's salary. It was a struggle, but I didn't have to get help from my parents or siblings. God sustained me, but I knew to keep paying my tithes and offerings. Through God, I made it. I was hoping and praying he would come back before anyone would have known that he left. Eventually, I did tell my parents in confidence. I still did not have the oral strength to tell my best friend or my siblings. As a matter of fact, my best friend and I went to Las Vegas for about seven or eight days and I still could not get the words out of my mouth to tell her that he was gone. She was and is a person that I could and can trust, but hurt and disappointment would not let me discuss it with her, even though she was and is a great prayer warrior. I remember her saying, "Let's send our husbands a postcard to our individual homes." But I knew my husband would never receive it because he was gone, gone.

I surely thought his leaving was to get my attention. He never told me he was unhappy or had other interests. He was just quiet and kept a lot on the inside. I was totally the opposite. I look back and realize that my personality was too strong for him. He was non-confrontational and the average man does not know how to communicate, so they get silent and go into a comatose mood. There I was thinking all was well, while he was keeping everything on the inside. He got to the point where he did not communicate his dislikes or unhappiness. He just showed me through leaving. That spoke more volumes than communicating. I would like to say to every reader that when you get married, stand before God, and recite those vows; you will be held accountable. I told my husband, when he came to get all of his belongings, that he made a vow to me and before God. I told him, if he leaves, he would reap. He told my dad that he needed a break, but he would be back. We already know that once Satan gets a true hold on you, there is no turning back for the most part. He stopped going to church. He stopped paying his tithes and offerings. He went down, down, down. But God blessed me to have more than ever than when it was both of our salaries.

I totally depended on God and no other man. I hid in God and in His Word. It manifested itself full circle. I made sure I stayed focused. I did not have a boyfriend, a handyman, or a play brother. I knew all those creatures bring on the lust of the flesh and lust of the eyes. I endured being alone and waiting on God. I can truly say like Naomi, "God who loves me, is better to me than seven sons or husbands." "And he shall be unto thee a restorer of thy life, and a nourisher of thine old age: for thy daughter in law, which loveth thee, which is better to thee than seven sons, hath born him." Ruth 4:15 "The Lord rewarded me according to my righteousness; according to the cleanness of my hands hath he recompensed me." Psalm 18:20

When my husband left me, for about two months, whenever I would open my Bible, it would always open up to the above scripture. I knew the Lord was speaking to me and giving me a message to keep my hands clean if I wanted to maintain his favor and his blessings. I have and will forever keep that on the table of my heart. When God speaks to you for two months with the same scripture, it means to take action and take heed. Also, it means Satan will set traps and tactics to trip you up. I was very leery of the opposite sex. Satan knows exactly what you like. He is going to send you exactly what you like to trick you. So that is why it is so important to tell God to guide and cover you. God will be our eye gates and anoint our eyes with eyesalve. "I counsel thee to buy of me gold tried in the fire, that thou mayest be rich; and white raiment, that thou mayest be clothed, and that the shame of thy nakedness do not appear; and anoint thine eyes with eyesalve, that thou mayest see." Revelation 3:18

In my dining room, there was dark, purple wallpaper. My furniture was cream with gold running through it. In my bathroom, there was dark burgundy wallpaper with golf clubs running through it and a gentleman. I live on a golf course, backed up to a lake. Those color schemes did not go with my furniture. I like light-colored walls throughout my home, so it would not look drab and unfriendly on rainy days and winter evenings and nights. So I went to Lowe's to buy the proper tools to remove wallpaper. Meanwhile, as I was leaving the store, one of the employees said, "If you need a painter, call me." So I took his name and number. I contacted him and I found out that this gentleman was very talented in building a house from the ground up. He could also rebuild and paint cars. He had various skill sets which contributed to making and designing a home. He was the gentleman I needed in moving into my new home. He came to my home, removed the wallpaper, replaced sheetrock, molding, replaced toilets and faucets, and painted the walls. I admired his God-given talent. He even put in a cedar closet for me. Anything I needed done, he did it for just pennies. It was unbelievable. I would always try to offer him more money, but he refused to take it. Therefore, I would use another strategy and ask him about his children, since he had introduced them to me. I would tell him to take it home to his children. That went over well every time.

He was a perfectionist. Things I would have thought nothing of, he wanted it to be perfectly done. So if a job was only for a week, it would take him a week and a half. I got tired of this. I knew my big buffet or china closet would be there in about three weeks. He was a long way from completing it. My sister, my best friend, and I began to pray that he would finish up soon. God put the running in his feet and hands. He was complete with everything before my buffet arrived from Mexico to California. He completed everything, and it was beautiful. He also did excellent work for my mom and my brother.

Come to find out, he had a hidden agenda. He was charging me very little money in hopes that we could become boyfriend and girlfriend. I did not know that at the time. Number one, I was still waiting for my husband to come back; And number two, he was not my type. I was sold out to God and kept my eyes stayed on Him. I was very innocent. I would put the alarm on and leave him at my home because he was trustworthy. He never came on to me and did not talk trash to me. He was very respectful. I even felt comfortable taking a bath upstairs while he was downstairs working. God gives us wisdom. I had the TV up and only had the water running when he ran his loud machine. Goodness and mercy were with me. "There shall no evil befall thee neither shall any plague come nigh thy dwelling. For he shall give his angels charge over thee, to keep in all thy ways. They shall bear thee up in their hands, lest thou dash thy foot against a stone." Psalm 91:10-12

My friends would tell me that they knew he had an interest in me. I did not notice until he had completed all his work for me. I would call him and text him. He never answered. I would do it extra early and extra late. He still would not pick up the phone or respond to my texts. I realized then, he wanted to have a relationship, but I did not play my hand. He was trying to win me over with kindness. He was just not my type. Not even for a friendship to eat hamburgers and fries. He was not my type. Not even to just chat on the phone casually. Again, he was very gifted, talented, skillful, and had a love for his mother and his two children. We were not compatible physically, financially, emotionally, spiritually, or naturally. After he saw that I was not interested, he never asked me out. He never asked could he call me, but he spoke volumes through other things. It was God who sent him away and would not let him answer the phone. His work was done over there. God will take down one and put up another. When you want to do right, God will bless you and open so many other doors.

After he completed the work for me, my neighbor next door became my extended help. I thank God for her. She was a lady with many degrees and a very prestigious job. She could work her professional job, be a wife, a mother, a grandmother, and an outstanding neighbor. She was given many, many gifts, such as a plumber, electrician, painter, and appliance fixer. She was like a genius in so many areas. God put her in my life. He placed me right next door to her on purpose. If you can name it, she can do it.

Her son has those same gifts as well. I lived next door to her for three years before I became cognizant of the gifts she possessed. I needed something small to be fixed. She fixed it like picking up a penny off the floor. I needed something medium fixed. She fixed it like picking up a nickel off the floor. And then one day, I needed something big to be fixed, so I asked her where I could get help to fix it. Of course, she replied, "I can fix it." And she did. She fixed it like picking up a dime off the floor. I stopped and asked her how she could do all of that without going to school for those trades. She said she inherited all of it from her grandmother, who could do all of that and would also get on the ground to work on cars. When her son would come home from school, he would be so embarrassed in front of his friends. Today, he sees the value of it and in it. He does the same things as his mother and his grandmother, but he had to go to school to be certified and licensed. I thank God that He put me next door to her, since I did not have a spouse or children. God has certainly looked out for me and took care of me over the years. I have lived in this home next door to her for 14 years now and she has saved me hundreds and thousands of dollars. I thank God for her, her talents, her gifts, and her skill sets. She is very phenomenal to me. I always would offer her money for her time, but she would never take it.

I can truly say, "In God I Trust." My neighbor has never charged me a penny for anything. God knew I did not have the money, but she enjoyed my company and having someone to vent to. When my husband passed and I received his benefits as a widow, I knocked on her door and showed her the reward letter of how much I would receive. She was so happy for me. I called her a few weeks later and told her I wanted to show her something. When I got there, I told her to hold her hand out, and I counted out so many benjamins. She told me she could not take that from me. I told her to buy her something big and special like some real diamond earrings. She still wears them to this day. I did this all because she has never taken anything for all she has done for me and my home. If you keep your hands clean, God will open doors to meet your needs.

We are helpers, one to another. A lot of times, when you bless people, God always blesses you to receive it back through other entities or people. In this case, I was glad to reciprocate, and she will still be blessed by God because she did it from her heart. She told me she did not feel right charging a neighbor, but I felt she needed to charge me, neighbor or not. I was calling and pulling on her like clockwork, so my best friend would give her gifts and money for birthdays, Christmases, and other special occasions. That really made her happy and put a smile on her face because my best friend thought a lot about her gifts and talents. That is what I love about God. When you live for Him, He will meet your needs with His riches and glory. I did not have to step out of holiness or righteousness, just for a man or a married man to help me in any shape, form, or fashion. God is definitely a provider. We as saints, Christians, or believers of Christ, do not have to bow nor bend to Satan for anything. "But my God shall supply all your need according to his riches in glory for Christ Jesus." Philippians 4:9

***

God gave me a seamstress, who was right at my fingertips to

take in and take up my clothes, from pajamas to my Sunday best. She really knew her work and was so professional. She had anointed hands. She did alterations for me, my best friend, and other ladies I've known for 17 consecutive years until she retired. She made our clothes look tailor-made. I thank God for her. We did not have to wear our clothes the way they were made, revealing everything. She would make special pieces, add snaps, zippers, etc. to keep us from being revealed. That is what I like about God. He is concerned about your concerns. God wants to play a part in every aspect of your life, not just the spiritual only. You know in Him, we live, move, and have our being. I try to take inventory of my life in the good, bad, and the ugly. It is all about connecting with God in everything. He wants to be first priority in our lives. In my 41-year walk with God, I have come to know the difference when someone acknowledges God in all that they do, and when they don't. The Bible says Peter got out of the boat on faith. Our whole walk with God is on faith because we have never seen Him. Peter walked on the water toward Jesus, by faith. As long as Peter kept his eyes on Jesus, Peter was fine. When Peter took his eyes off of Jesus, he saw the storm and began to sink. That is why it is imperative to keep God first in your life and in everything. The problem is that situations, unexpectancies, and disappointments, cannot take us out. We have to keep our eyes on Jesus, even in our minds. That is why we have perfect peace.

***

During all the years that I was without my husband, I never felt abandoned by God. I can truly say, like the poem *Footprints in the*

Sand, that it was the Lord who carried me and sustained me. You learn the Lord most through your adversities. You say, if it weren't for the Lord on my side, tell me where would I be? A lot of times, we only learn God through tests, trials, and tribulations. That is the time God is molding and making you. A lot of times, He is getting you ready for ministry. Some people think that ministry begins and ends in the pulpit. Real ministry is outside the four walls of the church. I did ministry through my teaching career, unbeknownst to me at the time. It just came naturally for me, through precept and example. It was so prevalent through my conduct, my dress, my walk, my talk, and my positive behavior. It had my students asking me about my belief and God. I knew the Law of Separation of church and state. Students have the right to ask and lead questions about faith, beliefs, and church. We as teachers could not initiate. A lot of my students followed me to church. So many of my students today are working in the church with leading roles; others are preaching and pastoring. I feel good as I am writing this book, knowing my living, teaching, and preaching were not in vain.

When I first started teaching, I was ashamed of promoting the gospel because it was not popular to do so, being young. "For whosoever shall be ashamed of me and of my words, of him shall the Son of man be ashamed when he shall come in his own glory, and in his Father's and of the holy angels." Luke 9:26 The more I would seek the face of God and read His Word, my courage began to strengthen and my faith increased. I felt like David in Psalms 18:29. I felt like I could run through a troop and leap over a wall in spreading the gospel. The more I studied the Word and taught Sunday school, my love for God began to increase and my boldness in Him began to rise, uncontrollably.

My siblings would try to criticize me and would say things like, "You can tell she was raised up in the church by the way she uses scripture." That was not cool to quote scripture. We already had to dress like we were sanctified and look like it too. How were we going to ever have a boyfriend or girlfriend? Our parents had already marked us from a child up. We did not have any room for escape unless we sneaked and did things, and we did. We had no peace because we were taught better, whereas our friends and peers did not have the teaching we did. Therefore, we could not cut up and sin in peace. My mother would tell us that. She made a believer out of me. My mother used to always tell us we were Israelites. Other children also knew we looked different, and we resented that with a passion because when you are in school, everybody wants to fit in. You do not want to stand out in an unpopular way, but a cool way.

We have all grown up and are very successful. None of that childish stuff matters anymore. It did back then, but we are all living for the Lord, proclaiming the Gospel. Two of my siblings are pastors, and my sister and I are ordained elders. My deceased sibling was an evangelist missionary. My eldest brother is in the church and loves Sunday school and testimony services. Our parents and my grandmother did an excellent job in raising us in the church and having family prayer and Bible study in the home. Man, how we resented it with a passion, but ask me how it paid off. It has kept us from a million failures.

Anyone who is rearing a family and would like for them as well as yourself to lead a peaceful life, you need to bring them up in church in the admonition of the Lord with urgency. Let them know you did not come to this world to live forever. You will die and stand in judgement before God. We are all soul winners. We all are born to do a work for God. It is our choice. He is not going to force it on us because God is a gentleman. These gifts were bestowed upon us at birth. "But the manifestation of the Spirit is given to every man to profit withal. For to one is given by the Spirit the word of wisdom; to another the word of knowledge by the same Spirit; To another faith by the same Spirit; to another the gifts of healing by the same Spirit; To another the working of miracles; to another prophecy; to another discerning of spirits; to another divers kinds of tongues; to another the interpretation of tongues" 1 Corinthians 12:7-10

The following are more gifts he has bestowed upon us. "And he gave some, apostles; and some, prophets; and some, evangelists; and some, pastors and teachers; For the perfecting of the saints, for the work of the ministry, for the edifying of the body of Christ." Ephesians 4:11-12

I thank God He has given me both natural and spiritual gifts. I remember that one of my math students had come to me crying from the doctor's report. She had been diagnosed with cancer and asked me would I pray for her. I wrote in detail about this earlier in the book. To sum it up, my student went back to the doctor and she had no signs of cancer.

God made a believer out of me and increased my faith. What a mighty God we serve! Gifts and callings come without repentance. Mind you, calling is as dynamic as gifts. God may choose to manifest a gift through someone over the span of a lifetime, and thereby, limit that person's calling to some specific task for life. God may also choose to manifest a gift for a particular time and place. God has done that several times in my life, far and in between.

***

My aunt had a terrible headache. I touched her head and prayed for her, and it left immediately. I prayed for a friend of mine's mother who could not walk. I didn't use any swelling words or speak in tongues. She began to walk. That is what I was referencing earlier when I said God sometimes chooses to manifest a gift for a particular time and place.

There are different things that I am experiencing in my body. I have laid hands on myself, prayed, and prayed. I have gone on long fasts. Nothing has changed. The situation is still the same. But I can say like Paul, God's grace is sufficient. God has given me the strength to endure. He has cooled the flames and lightened the load. Therefore, I know He is with me and He sees me. God has a set time for everything in our lives when we walk with Him and maintain a verbal and open relationship with him daily.

You definitely want to be on speaking terms with God, like you do with someone you love. That is what God wants even more because His Son gave His life for us, and God said He is a Jealous God, and Jealous is His name. "For the Lord thy God is a consuming fire, even a jealous God." Deuteronomy 4:24

"For thou shalt worship no other god: for the Lord, whose name is Jealous, is a jealous God." Exodus 34:14

***

I always tell the Lord that I do not want to do anything to let Him down. He has been so good to me. He's been better to me than I could be to myself. God has given me blessings that I knew I was not worthy of, definitely would not of, and could not even imagine. When I was growing up, I was just glad to receive a bachelor's degree. I never thought about going beyond that. That was like a doctorate degree to my little mind. Even though a lot of my colleagues had their master's degrees and were working in higher positions, I was so happy and felt so blessed with that one degree. One of my church members asked me if I was going back to school to get my master's. I humbly answered and said, "God is my Master." After that statement, God made a believer out of me, and my God, my Master, let me receive three more degrees. I received my master's degree and my Plus 45 degree for educators. God used a teacher on my job to help me in school to get my master's degree. First, she took me to dinner after school. She took me to the university, helped me to select what classes to take, what instructors to take, and what to do concerning tuition. Everything was so laid out and in place for me. The only thing I had to do was show up. I knew it was the Lord opening that door for me. It did not interfere with my teaching job, my church work, and neither of my church services. I basically made all A's. I was so happy and encouraged. God had given me favor with the professors.

I connected with a colleague who had gone to college with me, but we were not friends at the time. We became close friends, working on our masters. We took all of our classes together. We studied together. We influenced each other to get our Plus 45 degree. That is a degree that is 45 hours toward your doctorate if you decide to get one. Otherwise, if you do not, you will still get paid for it in your salary if you are a teacher. We were so happy to have earned three degrees under our belt. God blessed us mightily to write our thesis. I will tell anyone and suggest to anyone if you are furthering your education, to link up with someone. The task becomes easier because you have someone to share it with and mull over your ideas and thoughts.

We graduated. After our third degree, I got engaged and got married five months later. She was in my wedding. Afterwards, she went down her path in life and I went down my path in life. She called me about six years later and said she thought we should pursue our doctorate degree. I immediately said, yes! At this time, my husband had left me and I felt this would be a great distraction. Teaching school every day and working on my final degree, which was my doctorate, was perfect timing, or so I thought. I found a good program in Southern Illinois and she found a good program in Florida. She sent off for her paperwork and I sent off for mine. We wanted our acceptance letters. She received hers and so did I. We both knew we were on the right road. This would surely keep my mind off of my husband leaving me. I was more focused on, where do I go from here?

Well as I began to fill out my papers, I was so excited. My friend and I were at it again. Getting all of our degrees together and this last one, our doctorate. You know sometimes God will speak through people. Sometimes through prophecy. Sometimes through His Word. Sometimes He WILL SPEAK DIRECTLY to you. Well, this was a time, I could not get out of it and get around it. He told me as I was filling the papers, "DON'T GO!" I kept trying to reason and rationalize with God, but when He speaks, it is what it is. This was in 1994. I was so discouraged because BIG GOD did not give me an answer or a reason. I knew from reading the Word, we must obey God, and God never makes a mistake.

My friend went on to Florida State and started working on her degree. I soon got over it and went on with my life. I did not hear from her for a long time. We reconnected in 2000. God told me that I could then get my doctorate degree. I hit the ground running when I heard about this special program that was being offered. They looked at my resume, all my awards, accomplishments, and my many, many community works. All of that gave me so much credit toward my doctorate. I started at the beginning of 2003, and I marched eight months later in August with my doctoral degree. I see why God told me to wait and DON'T GO. He knew a special program would be coming up, and it would be less complicated for me to work full time and try to get my doctorate. When God speaks, we may not know the outcome, but we will understand it by and by. At this point, my friend still did not have her degree. I helped her with the dissertation, and she graduated right after me with her Ph.D. We still received all of our degrees together. God still had us there for each other. She got married and I was also in her wedding. God gives you a friend for several reasons. Some for a season. Some forever. Some for a reason. Our relationship was for a reason and a season. God gives and blesses us with things that we know not of because He is a faithful God.

***

I had this church friend who loved New York and wanted to expose her young ladies at the church to the New York experience and all its energy. They went every year during the public school's spring break, and they asked me if I would be their tour guide. I was delighted and excited because I knew New York like I knew my own hometown. I knew all the streets that were good for tourists. I knew all the nice restaurants. I knew about Broadway plays and off-Broadway plays. I introduced them to Harlem, Queens, Staten Island, the Statue of Liberty, the Empire State Building, the Apollo theatre, Malcolm Shabazz Avenue, the Waldorf Astoria, 5th Avenue, China Town, Canale Street, 5-star restaurants, Central Park, Windows on the World, and Tavern on the Green. They flew me into Laguardia, seven years in a row, and paid for my hotels and most of my meals. Your gifts will make room for you. "A many gifts maketh room for him and brigeth him before great men." Proverbs 18:16

***

When I moved into my new home, I wanted to have a housewarming because I wanted everyone to see how the Lord had blessed me with my first home without the aid or assistance from my husband. But God told me clearly, do not have a housewarming. Sometimes when God speaks to us we are not sure if it's him or not. Is it just a thought? Is this my conscience or what? But there are other times God makes it perfectly clear. "This is Me and Only Me. Do not have a housewarming." I just could not understand that either, but as the old adage says, "You will understand by and by."

My friend had been saving up for her new home, year after year.

The Lord spoke to her and told her to give me her things and He would bless her. But before that, she had told her siblings, she had a lot of things she'd been saving for her new home and they were welcomed to come and get what they wanted. They all said they were coming, but they never got around to it. They had excuse after excuse. When she said she was going to give it to me, they all started hollering, "I want it, I want it!" What God has for you is for you. My friend, who is an interior decorator, came to my home and told me she had so many decors that would fit in well with my color scheme. Everything else, like floral arrangements, she made it for every room. That was nobody but God. Then God told me why I did not need a housewarming party because I would receive a lot of things that I was already equipped with, like sheets, towels, toasters, kitchen gadgets, etc. I have more than enough of those things. I needed floral arrangements, sconces, wall pictures, bathroom fixtures, decorations for the foyer, sunroom, catwalk, and porch. She GAVE me all of that and did not charge me for one picture. God told her what she gives me, she would get back and more. God is about to bless her in a miraculous way that man could not do, but God could, but that's another whole chapter in my book or hers. When people come into my home, the first thing they ask is, "Who decorated your home?" They could see that it was professionally done. When God gives you an order or a directive, oftentimes, you cannot put all the pieces of the puzzle together. But one day, you will, and the puzzle is all connected in the right place.

God wants us to trust Him in everything and wait on Him. Even when we cannot trace Him, He wants us to trust Him. The more we do these things, our faith increases and we get to learn Him and be able to tell others about Him, just as I'm doing in this book. The song says, *If I did not have a problem, I would not know God could solve them, but through it all I've learned to trust in Jesus. I've learned to trust His Word.*

***

When my dad died after being married to my mother for 61 years, his death devastated my mom and us. They did everything together. So when he left to be with the Lord, part of her left as well, physically and mentally. We were all well into our careers and my other sister lived out of town. We did not know who was going to keep my mom, live with my mom, cook for my mom, or be her constant companion until she went home to be with the Lord. We tried several people from the church, but that did not work out. But God had a ram in the bush, and that was one of our childhood friends who grew up with us in the church. Our parents also fellowshipped with her. We sang with her on the radio and her mother carried us to church events and activities. She was no stranger to us or my mother.

We had lost fellowship with her and she had stepped out in the world. But when God has a plan for your life, no devil can keep it from prospering. Our childhood friend came to our church one Sunday in February and gave her life to God, and we got her to attend prayer meetings three times a week, so she could put on spiritual strength and be around seasoned and strong saints. She was used to the worldly culture and its lifestyle, but now she had to get in tune with the spiritual and kingdom culture.

My brother took off 90 days FMLA and took her to prayer

meetings along with our mother. He was helping them spiritually and he was being helped spiritually. She began to grow spiritually and enjoyed the things of God and began to take my mother every Tuesday night to a downtown church. She would look forward to this every week, and my mother would, too. She enjoyed the preached word from the Bishop and she would have something to feast on throughout the week. She would tell different people how she was so encouraged and how the Word gave her strength to take on her new role as a caregiver.

We were so happy and relieved for the plan of God and how He worked that situation out. Our caregiver had a home to live in and she was in charge. Her only task was to take care of our mom and cook for her. We paid every bill that came to that house. We paid her a very good salary every two weeks, too.

God had magnificently blessed me. All the pieces of the puzzle were finally coming together. My siblings and I were able to maintain our careers and carry on the work of the Lord at our churches. My sister sent approximately $500 monthly to my mom for any needed expense. She realized she did not live here and she was not able to help with our mom physically, so she kept her money coming monthly and never missed a payment. She would give the caregiver money when she would go on trips. My sister really honored our mother, although she lived out of town.

When she would come to visit, she played intricate parts in taking care of my mom and going out to dinner with her. Mind you, my mom was up in age with dementia. She could not hold a stable-minded conversation. My sister loved her anyway and came to see her until she died 11 years after my dad's death. Our caregiver was glad to be in charge of my mom's home with all the bills paid. She had all the weekends and holidays off. She was able to drive several luxury cars and build her credit score up to 796. Therefore, she was able to lease a car every three years.

I took my caregiver and my mom to Michigan to visit my sister. We had a nice flight. Sometimes my mother would not cooperate with us when going through security and riding in elevators. God gave us the strength to work with my mom and to dress her nicely. She had the best of everything since my dad was gone. I gave her several flights out of town. I bought her another mink coat, new dentures, wigs, pearls, a seasonal wardrobe, and holiday clothes. I did for my mom, as if she had all the faculties of her mind, mainly, because she gave us the best. I wanted and we wanted her to have the best. We're supposed to honor our mother and father, regardless of whatever frame of mind they have.

***

God has always blessed me with extraordinary favor. My best friends paid for my manicures for two consecutive years.

The school I was teaching in had a cosmetology course and God gave me favor with the instructor. She did my hair free every two weeks. I offered to pay her even though I did not have extra money. She refused to take anything. She said she enjoyed doing my hair and it was her pleasure. That was nobody but God. I had an hour and a half free every day. She would do it all in that length of time.

During Christmas, I charged a very pricey gift for her at Macy's. She was so happy. I was glad to make her heart happy since she made me happy, even though she did not know my financial situation. Again, God covered me.

***

I once had a student in my classroom that did not do well in school and always had problems with the teachers she had. Some kind of way, she took a liking to me and respected me. The other colleagues recognized that. When they had problems with her, they would send her to my classroom. Her grandmother gave me a gas card to use for six months. I did not abuse it. It caused me to be humbled. That wasn't anybody but God proving Himself strong on my behalf.

***

My best friend, her husband, and aide, took turns buying my dinner every Friday and Sunday for about a year. They even paid for my monthly medications. If I did not go out to eat with them every Friday, they would literally be upset and disappointed, whereas I thought that would give them a break on their wallet. They were not looking at it that way.

That was God, again, smiling on me.

***

I have always been able to lease luxury cars every three years. God gave me outstanding favor with the owner. He would always put money in my hand and my best friend's hand. He would fill our cars with gas, and whenever he would see us, he would give us money. That was nobody but God. All of my cars would have all the bells and whistles. I would always drive one of the most glamourous cars in the city.

***

When my dad was pastoring the church, I was always an advocate of him and a promoter. I would always execute his agenda, whether I thought it was idealistic or not. It is the same way with my brother, who was his successor. I tell you, God has and is rewarding me for my works. Again, I did everything in the church before I received my license and being ordained; from teaching Sunday school to being a pallbearer. The only thing I have not done in ministry, is baptized someone.

***

God blessed me to become a millionaire twelve years ago. He specifically gave me who to share the money with. I gave out three hundred and forty thousand dollars to 66 people and gave them a millionaire party the weekend leading up to Labor Day. I sent out invitations, not telling them what they were coming to. I just told them to come dressed up and empty-handed. Most people thought I was inviting them to a surprise wedding. They had all kinds of thoughts, but they never thought they would be attending an affair, and leaving from it loaded with thousands of dollars, with no strings attached or will ever have to pay back. Well, it was reality. God chose me to be the steward over the money, who to share it with, and how much to give each one. When I did my presentation to each one, I gave them an envelope with a check inside and told them to meet me at the bank at 9:00 a.m.

So many people were crying and screaming, and the food went to waste. They had lost their appetites. Some were dancing and some were running. This is what I told everyone when I gave them the envelope. "When God blessed me, He was thinking of you." I thank God to this day that He could trust me to distribute and dispense liberally and not grudgingly. Whenever God blesses anyone with an overflow, it is to share. It is not for "my four and no more" and "me, myself, and I." It will surely flow through your hands like water, and it will seem as if your pockets have holes in them.

The Lord told me, through prophecy, that the amount of money He is going to bless me with in the future will be no comparison to what He gave me. Some people like to keep quiet about the money God has blessed them with because they do not want to share one red cent. Some people get nasty attitudes when they receive big money. My brother has always said, and I have witnessed it, that money magnifies who a person really is. If you are a fool without money, you are an even bigger fool with money. "A fool and his money are soon parted." Proverbs 21:20

The more the Lord has blessed us with, the more humble we should be. This is not the time to brag, boast, show off on Facebook, promote yourself, or go around people so they can see you. God is number one. It is all about Him. We are free moral agents, but we are to promote God at all times and lift up JESUS. It is all about Him, not the lust of the eyes, the lust of the flesh, and the pride of life. Be encouraged and Be Blessed.

***

I remember one of my best friends from high school asked me

to lend her a thousand dollars for her earnest money to go with the signing of her contract for her new home. I was more than glad to do it. She was a very nice young lady and my family members loved her. I went to the bank near the school I was working in and took out a signature loan of a thousand dollars. I got the money and gave it to her. She paid me back just as she promised, leading up to Christmas, and the way I wanted it- "all cash." She brought it to my job and gave me 10 one hundred dollar bills. My sister taught me to always secure my money in my top undergarment in a pouch. I did not know she was securing the pouch with a safety pin. I did the same thing, but I did not secure it with a pin.

It was the Christmas holidays coming up and I was so busy getting my Christmas decorations ready for the school's Christmas program and wrapping boxes. I would constantly bend forward to pick this up and pick that up, not knowing my money was making its way out of my undergarment. The students were working very closely with me, but they swore and declared they did not see the money fall or anyone picking it up. We went back over all my tracks, even in the rain. No one saw it but God. So I gave up. Only God would make those students tell me the truth. It was Christmas time. They probably hid it and divided it among themselves and said, "She has money. She's not going to miss it. She doesn't have any children to spend it on. She will never miss it." The whole thing was a mystery. I knew my friend did pay me and she paid me in cash. I went to the bank just to see. Did I really take the money out? I knew I did because I had the receipt. The clerk looked at my account and told me that I never took the thousand dollars out and I never borrowed it. Well, I had witnesses that I did: God, the young lady who is living in the home today who borrowed the earnest money, the lady at the bank who generated the receipt, and myself.

My dad told me to give them 90 days, and they will see their mistake. It is 24 years later, and I never paid that thousand dollars back, nor did my students find the 10 one hundred dollar bills that fell out of my clothes. My friend girl felt so bad because she said, "If you would have taken a check, this would not have happened." That is so true. In the end, we all received the victory. My friend girl moved into her new home. I did not have to pay the bank back. And we said maybe someone at school must have really, really needed it for Christmas. A good time was had by all. God is so amazing and He is still working miracles. Only God will do that.

***

I remember when I purchased my new home for $300,000, all I had was faith and a good credit score. My realtor told me that with my excellent credit score and how the stock market was trending, I could qualify for the home, but my salary would not afford the home by myself because of the monthly mortgage. "But God," the Big He, sustained me.

My financier told me that I would be able to get the home because of my credit score and the market was down and the banks were at an all-time low and loss. He said that I would not be able to pay the monthly mortgage. I heard him but did not hear him. I never made a major purchase that required that kind of money, so I had no inkling of what he was saying. But time will take you on. I did not have the salary to move into that home. Sometimes it is good to be green. That is when God can really work.

At that time, I was only making $50,000 a year and trying to purchase a home for $300,000! What was I thinking? Did I learn anything about math while I was teaching students for 35 years? Did I want the beautiful home so badly that it fogged my common sense? Maybe I had the faith of a mustard seed. Yeah, that had to be the answer. I did buy the home on faith. I went to closing without a dollar. Just dumb and naïve. When I got to closing, they told me to give them a check for $1,200. That amount shocked me so much. Even now, I cannot tell you what that $1,200 was for. I just knew I did not have the small amount of $12.00, not to mention $1,200! Everyone at the table could look at me and tell something was wrong with me mentally and that I must have had severe issues. Nevertheless, my realtor spoke up for me and said, "The selling of this home is a benefit to everyone in this room. Let us all divide the $1,200 four ways and help her pay it." They all wrote a check and paid it. I still was in la-la-land. Everything was happening so fast toward me. When they told me my monthly mortgage was going to be $2,346.83, I could have run out of that room like the lion did on the Wizard of Oz. What helped me to sit in that room feeling like I was in trance, but not looking like it, was that I had just come off a 30-day fast concerning my new home. I never could have imagined living on a golf course backed up to a lake in a gated community.

That life was only afforded to the type of people with six-figure incomes. I moved into that home, which previously belonged to a medical doctor that had his house custom-made for him and ME. God had me in mind when that house was built. Every custom item I wanted and dreamed of was in this house: an all-white kitchen with an island and double bedroom suites. I have 27 windows, 12 of which are overlooking a lake and a golf course. God helped me up and gave me the victory. I have been living here for 14 years and have a credit score of 849, paying my mortgage from my deceased husband's social security disability. "Ain't God Alright!" God kept telling me for the cleanness of my hands, He will bless me. I had to keep my hands clean to keep and maintain the upkeep of this house. I went through a lot, I must not leave out, but God saw me through and put people in my life to see me through. God said in His Word, He will not make you ashamed. You must have clean hands when you step out on faith to that kind of magnitude.

The Lord blessed my mom, her caregiver, and me. One day as I was driving and entering the freeway, an elderly man rear-ended the back of my car. The impact was very great. However, we did not have any pain, soreness, or discomfort down the road. The caregiver looked at me, my mom, and herself and said, "Guess What? All of our wigs are off our heads." I said, "For real?" Then I looked in the mirror and mine was completely off and on the floor. My mom's wig was completely off and on the seat, and so was the caregiver's wig. Again, the impact was so hard and quick, it knocked us into a shock. God shielded us. We could have lost each other, just like that. With that kind of impact to take our wigs off of our heads, the same impact could have broken our necks. Death and hell are in God's hands. That was not our death date. We walked and drove away with the victory. We went to church that night and really praised the Lord for life. He gave us another chance. Many people we know who were our age are already dead and gone. But God saw fit for us to live on. God is truly in control of everything and everybody in this universe. Nothing happens unless He allows it. I know I am still here because I have work to do for the Lord. My sentiment is that I will fulfill the purpose He has for me. That is my purpose for life and in life.

***

One day downtown, I saw the gentleman from Lowe's who worked on my house. He yelled out from across the street and spoke to me. I also ran into him again at a fast-food restaurant. He sat beside me and we chatted. My roommate was with me, and he told her, so I could hear him, that he wanted to date me. I exclaimed in a jovial way, "You are not my type." He probably thought, this is 10 years later, and you are yet without your husband. He didn't know my husband had died, neither was I going to make him aware. As I said before, I had no chemistry with him, not even as a friend. Some people in life, you like as a friend for sundry reasons. Some friendships blossom into other things that are not of God and are not sanctioned by God. That is why in all our ways we must acknowledge God in everything and every day. When you wake up and pray, you ask the Lord to order your steps and endorse you, in His son Jesus's name. God will snatch us from the snare of the enemy like David said in Psalm 25. Anyone that does not have God as their personal Savior and a one-on-one, day-to-day relationship and fellowship with Him, you are living beneath your privileges. God can do anything but fail. Everything belongs to God, even the cattle on a thousand hills. "For every beast of the forest is mine, and the cattle upon a thousand hills." Psalm 50:10

***

I thank God for all the friends he has placed in my life since childhood. My three friends, who were my best friends since junior high, are still fellowshipping and corresponding today, from 12 years old until now. We still visit each other and go on lunch and dinner dates. Then God gave me another best friend that I grew up with in the same church since we were five years old. We have been living together for the last five years. She is 63 and I am 64 years old. She took care of my mom and ran her home for 11 years. When my mom passed on to glory, we sold her home. I told her she could come and live with me. She lives on the main floor with a very large master suite, and I live on the second floor with a very large master suite. We both have our very own space and privacy. God blessed that the home is big, with two refrigerators. It has a custom-made refrigerator and a traditional refrigerator. She has her own and I have my own. God knows our beginning and our ending, and of course, the in-between. She is not lacking or wanting anything and neither am I. We have five bathrooms. We take turns paying for the home to be cleaned. She carries her own weight. She is not a freeloader or a moocher. She stands on her own two feet. When God ordains something, all the pieces of the puzzle will fit. I had two other friends who were in my life since our childhood; they silently passed away. One of them left her daughter in my hands. She has been my goddaughter for forty years. I also have two friends in the ministry who have prayed and played intricate parts in my life. One has been my best friend for 20 years and the other has been my best friend for over 32 years. It makes a difference when God ordains a relationship with friends. Come what may, through hell or high water, it will stand.

***

The friend that is and has been in my life for 32 years, our bond came from a true foundation and that was on our knees in prayer meetings all across the city. We have the same spiritual goal and mission. Our goal is to make it to heaven to see Jesus and to live with Him and the Father. Our mission is that our life will cause others to see Jesus in our lives and become followers of Him. We have traveled abroad and gone overseas and have done great missionary work for the Lord. We gave our time, talent, and treasures. We have traveled to over 10 countries, some of the countries are in the Bible. We even went to the Isle of Patmos where John was sent. We traveled to Mars Hill and had service there. It is the same location as one of Paul's most important gospel presentations he presented during his visit to Athens during his second missionary journey. God blessed us to go on a huge cruise line ship to Greece. God blessed us to purchase a mink coat in Greece at the mink factory.

***

I thank God for all the trips to New York and abroad in the UK. We always started our day off in prayer, 30 minutes to an hour, and ended it the same way before we went to bed. God would give us much favor with people in shopping and eating out. I was given the chance by God to introduce a Muslim man to Christianity. He did not want to let me go. We were in Australia when God gave me this witnessing experience. He told me he could not leave the Muslim faith because his entire family was in it. I told him to pray to God and the Lord to show him the way out and be sincere and God would do exactly that. We embraced each other and went our separate ways. Is he a Christian today? I do not know. I know I planted the seed; God will send someone else to water it, and God will do the increase. "I have planted, Apollos watered; but God gave the increase. So then neither is he that planteth any thing, neither he that watereth; but God that giveth the increase. Now he that planteth and he that watereth are one: and every man shall receive his own reward according to his own labour." I Corinthians 3:6-8 God knows who are is. "And other sheep I have, which are not of this fold: them also I must bring, and they shall hear my voice; and there shall be one fold, and one shepherd." John 10:16

I knew to pray for him and his family daily. I will keep them on my prayer list. Prayer is far-reaching and prayer changes things. That man had a very sincere heart, but I can tell by the things he was telling me, he felt like he was stuck between a rock and a hard place. We know there is nothing too hard for God. Man's extremity is God's opportunity. God wants to make believers out of us.

***

There would be times in my life when I was going through tests and trials. I would sit at the edge of the bed and say, "Where is God?" I knew where God was. He was sitting on the throne and seeing what was going on. We are earthlings, and we are impatient, and we look for God to right every wrong immediately because we know He has all power; therefore, we feel we should not want for anything. God forbids. If God would come to our rescue every time something happens in our lives, we would not honor Him, pray, fast, or worship Him. We will treat Him as a good Charlie or henpeck. God knows how much we can bear. He knows how to keep us humble. He sets the limits when our tests begin and when our tests end. Some tests are popcorn tests. They pop up, then all of a sudden from nowhere, it is over. You assess what has happened and realize that was a test for me and I failed it. I overreacted. I handled it wrongly. I could have been nicer about it. I failed that test. I have to go through that again. God wanted me to see myself. The next time I am going to be more watchful and prayerful. I should have humbled myself and taken the high road. I should have let God fight my battle. I should have studied to be quiet. "And that ye study to be quiet, and to do your own business, and to work with your own hands, as we commanded you." 1 Thessalonians 4:11

God wants us to see ourselves the way He sees us. Therefore, the Bible says, "Every way of a man is right in his own eyes, but the Lord pondereth the hearts. To do justice and judgment is more acceptable to the LORD than sacrifice." Proverbs 21:2-3

***

Even when we are not in a test or going through a trial, we need to take inventory of our lives. We need to ask ourselves, "Is the Lord satisfied with me? Can anyone see Christ in my life? Am I a living epistle or an ambassador for Christ?" The Bible says we are more than conquerors. We have the victory. "Thou art my battle ax and weapons of war: for with thee will I break in pieces the nations, and with thee will I destroy kingdoms; And with thee will I break in pieces the horse and his rider; and with thee will I break in pieces the chariot and his rider; With thee also will I break in pieces man and woman; and with thee will I break in pieces old and young; and with thee will I break in pieces the young man and the maid; I will also break in pieces with thee the shepherd and his flock; and with thee will I break in pieces the husbandman and his yoke of oxen; and with thee will I break in pieces captains and rulers." Jeremiah 51:20-23 Now if we are God's battle ax, then we are His weapons of warfare. The Lord wants us to destroy many Pharaohs today. He is looking for the Moses that will serve as His instrument of battle in His hands and the vehicle that carries His Word. Ask yourself, "Am I One in Jesus's name?"

***

As I told you earlier, different ones would prophesy to me, "He'll be back." I believed the several ones who prophesied this to me. Then, others would prophesy that I would be getting married again. I rejected that prophecy immediately. Well, both sets of prophecies and prophets were correct. When they told me he'll be back, I took it upon myself to believe they were talking about my husband. No one called the name of the "He." I just assumed, and they probably assumed as well. But we know the "He" could not have been him, because he passed in 2016.

The Lord revealed to me who the "He" was. "He" was a gentleman that I dated approximately 41 years ago. As we know, so much water has gone over the dam. I hadn't seen or heard anything about this gentleman anymore other than that he was doing well, married with four beautiful children, and was called to the ministry.

A man of the cloth. I never ran into him like my other friends. I never thought to look him up on Facebook because I did not have any interests. But when God has a set time for something to be, it is going to be.

It was January 2018, the last Saturday of the month. I was on a 40-day fast. My roommate and I were in prayer, and one of my siblings called and told me to take the number of an old friend from the early '80s. He told me his name and immediately said I remembered him. My sibling said he was at a funeral, and he came up and told him who he was and detained him for about 20 – 30 minutes, going down memory lane of our entire family, calling everyone by name. He also told him about the church we attended back then. He told him about our mother and father. He said he had been looking for me for over 40 years to say thank you for saving his life. He told me when we were dating that I had left the classroom and went to the office and called him. He said when the phone rang, that woke him up because his entire house was engulfed with thick smoke. He had left a pot on the stove and had fallen asleep. He had just worked the 11-7 shift, came home, thinking a quick power nap would be sufficient enough for whatever was cooking to be ready about the time the power nap was over. The power nap overtook him and it became a real nighttime sleep. He said if I had not called him, he would have died from smoke inhalation.

The fire department came, took over his home, and he escaped. At that time, he was in his twenties. Since he has gotten older, he appreciates life and how God shielded and protected him back then. He said he would pass my old family home, hoping he would see me because his company FedEx was right up the street. He said when he would pass by the Pine Hill Golf Course, he would think about me so deeply for saving his life. For over forty years, he wished he could see me or run into me so he could tell me, "Thank you." My brother said he could not get rid of him. He just stood there talking about me and our family and about what happened 40 years ago. He just wanted me to call him, so he could thank me. My brother said he was so polite, patient, and well dressed as he took pictures after the funeral was over. My brother likes to take pictures everywhere he goes. Taking pictures is his hobby as well as a passion for him. He said he only went to the funeral to support his son's brother. He didn't know anyone there; neither did he know the deceased. But as the Bible says, "And he must needs go through Samaria." John 4:4 My brother was destined to go to that funeral so my long-lost friend could see him and connect with me over 40 years later.

He liked how the gentleman did not ask for my number but left his instead. I got excited to hear all of this, like a 16-year-old girl. I don't know why because I hadn't seen or heard from him in four decades plus. So what was the big deal! I got the courage and boldness to call him. He had the very same voice he had 40 years ago. He told me he passed my parent's home many times, going to work, hoping he would see me. He said he went on Facebook hoping he could find me but he did not know my married name. He said there has never been a year that has gone by that he did not think about me. He had gone to the church my brother pastored but did not feel comfortable asking about me or asking him to have me call him.

What God has for you, it is for you. So the Lord gave him another chance to run into my brother again. We connected that Saturday by way of telephone. He told me to send him some pictures of myself and he would send me pictures of him. Of course, I sent nothing but glamour shots and he did the same. He said he had been married but has been separated for over six years. I told him I'd been married and my husband had been deceased for three years. He asked if he could come over after church so we could see each other. I said yes because I would be coming from church and I would have my church clothes on. This would be the ideal time.

So, he came in a navy blue BMW sports car with all the bells and whistles. It was clean, shining, and the rims were beautiful. But the man who was driving it stood out more than the car! He rang the doorbell. In walked this medium tall, slim, dark brown complexion man. He was well-groomed from head to toe. It seemed as if he had just come off the runway. The skin on his face was tight. His glasses were so becoming to him. His suit fit him to a T. The cufflinks were so stunning. The cuffs on his shirts were so neat and white. His bowtie fit so perfectly under his neck. His checkered shirt was the perfect match for his bowtie and pocket square. His shoes were shined so professionally. His socks were neat on his ankles. His fingernails were well-kempt. His mustache was edged perfectly. As the saying goes, he did not have a fly on him anywhere. He looked as if he was dressed for the White House or Hollywood. I was so impressed with his outward appearance. I could tell God had been good to him. If I had met him on the street or in the mall, I never would have known it was him. Back then, he was taller, with a giant afro, and kind of built. Now he has a few frazzles on his head and slimmer, but he was so, so handsome to me. The only thing I could recognize about him was his voice. His voice was still the same and distinguished. I absolutely loved what I saw.

As we started to talk about his four children, I could tell he had a very special love for his children individually. I could tell he was a family man that promoted education and salvation. His three daughters were extremely beautiful and shapely. His oldest daughter was born when he was only 20, but it was still so beautiful to me how he kept up with her and helped her through college. She is very much a part of his other three children's lives. She comes home for the holidays and any big events. He goes and visits her out of town if she doesn't feel well. He talked about his son, who is very handsome and named after him. He played his video for me to see. I can tell he is a good father who invested a lot in his children. I admired that because my father was outstanding and gave us everything to make it in this world. From the belt to the Bible was the way he raised us. My siblings and I are holding on to their teachings with both hands and teeth. We cherished every discipline, prayer meeting, Bible study, everyday living, and teachings. If every parent or parents would rear their children at an early age, showing them love through the belt and the Bible, we would have a better and peaceful world.

My friend had a good job with outstanding benefits from a reputable company. He was now an ordained minister. He had such a beautiful life, but a shattered marriage. God knows how to keep us humble and praying. He was such a classy gentleman. It was something for me to witness that night, some 40 years later. I have seen a lot of my old friends, but none of them struck my attention like this one did. He had the persona, the professional attire, the spiritual look, he quoted scriptures verbatim, he was family-oriented, he loved his mom, and visited her every day until she died. God answered his prayers. He told the Lord that he did not want anyone to call him and tell him his mother had passed. He wanted to be there during her passing, and God honored that for him. He had everything going for him that my parents would approve of. The Lord let me know that this is the "He'll Be Back" that everybody prophesied about. Have I ever told him? No. Have I ever let on to him? No. God has just given me a glimpse of the future. God has a set date and time in heaven. I am not in a rush. I just want to be in God's perfect will and not his permissive will. Forty some years later, he found me. We both are doing well, financially stable, but we had shattered marriages. Only God knows where we will go from here. I do not want to get in God's way or His plans. I just want to stand still and see the salvation of the Lord. I have the F.A.I.T.H. "For All I Trust Him."

Chapter 10

The Indifferent Kept Me Listening to God

I thank God for having and knowing the Word down on the inside. It comforts me during my trying times and lonely hours. Whenever I would open up the Bible, it would already be turned to Psalm 18. God would give it to me to read in its entirety. If the Bible was not turned to Psalm 18, the Lord would lead me to 2 Samuel 22. Psalm 18:1-50 says, "¹I will love thee, O Lord, my strength. ²The Lord is my rock, and my fortress, and my deliverer; my God, my strength, in whom I will trust; my buckler, and the horn of my salvation, and my high tower. ³ I will call upon the Lord, who is worthy to be praised: so shall I be saved from mine enemies. ⁴ The sorrows of death compassed me, and the floods of ungodly men made me afraid. ⁵ The sorrows of hell compassed me about: the snares of death prevented me. ⁶ In my distress I called upon the

Lord, and cried unto my God: he heard my voice out of his temple, and my cry came before him, even into his ears. [7] Then the earth shook and trembled; the foundations also of the hills moved and were shaken, because he was wroth. [8] There went up a smoke out of his nostrils, and fire out of his mouth devoured: coals were kindled by it. [9] He bowed the heavens also, and came down: and darkness was under his feet. [10] And he rode upon a cherub, and did fly: yea, he did fly upon the wings of the wind. [11] He made darkness his secret place; his pavilion round about him were dark waters and thick clouds of the skies. [12] At the brightness that was before him his thick clouds passed, hail stones and coals of fire. [13] The Lord also thundered in the heavens, and the Highest gave his voice; hail stones and coals of fire. [14] Yea, he sent out his arrows, and scattered them; and he shot out lightnings, and discomfited them. [15] Then the channels of waters were seen, and the foundations of the world were discovered at thy rebuke, O Lord, at the blast of the breath of thy nostrils. [16] He sent from above, he took me, he drew me out of many waters. [17] He delivered me from my strong enemy, and from them which hated me: for they were too strong for me. [18] They prevented me in the day of my calamity: but the Lord was my stay. [19] He brought me forth also into a large place; he delivered me, because he delighted in me. [20] The Lord rewarded me according to my righteousness; according to the cleanness of my hands hath he recompensed me. [21] For I have kept the ways of the Lord, and have not wickedly departed from my God. [22] For all his judgments were before me, and I did not put away his statutes from me. [23] I was also upright before him, and I kept myself from mine iniquity. [24] Therefore hath the Lord recompensed me according to my righteousness, according to the cleanness of my hands in his eyesight. ²⁵ With the merciful thou wilt shew thyself merciful; with an upright man thou wilt shew thyself upright; ²⁶ With the pure thou wilt shew thyself pure; and with the froward thou wilt shew thyself froward. ²⁷ For thou wilt save the afflicted people; but wilt bring down high looks. ²⁸ For thou wilt light my candle: the Lord my God will enlighten my darkness. ²⁹ For by thee I have run through a troop; and by my God have I leaped over a wall. ³⁰ As for God, his way is perfect: the word of the Lord is tried: he is a buckler to all those that trust in him. ³¹ For who is God save the Lord? or who is a rock save our God? ³² It is God that girdeth me with strength, and maketh my way perfect. ³³ He maketh my feet like hinds' feet, and setteth me upon my high places. ³⁴ He teacheth my hands to war, so that a bow of steel is broken by mine arms. ³⁵ Thou hast also given me the shield of thy salvation: and thy right hand hath holden me up, and thy gentleness hath made me great. ³⁶ Thou hast enlarged my steps under me, that my feet did not slip. ³⁷ I have pursued mine enemies, and overtaken them: neither did I turn again till they were consumed. ³⁸ I have wounded them that they were not able to rise: they are fallen under my feet. ³⁹ For thou hast girded me with strength unto the battle: thou hast subdued under me those that rose up against me. ⁴⁰ Thou hast also given me the necks of mine enemies; that I might destroy them that hate me. ⁴¹ They cried, but there was none to save them: even unto the Lord, but he answered them not. ⁴² Then did I beat them small as the dust before the wind: I did cast them out as the dirt in the streets. ⁴³ Thou hast delivered me from the strivings of the people; and thou hast made me the head of the heathen: a people whom I have not known shall serve me. [44] As soon as they hear of me, they shall obey me: the strangers shall submit themselves unto me. [45] The strangers shall fade away, and be afraid out of their close places. [46] The Lord liveth; and blessed be my rock; and let the God of my salvation be exalted. [47] It is God that avengeth me, and subdueth the people under me. [48] He delivereth me from mine enemies: yea, thou liftest me up above those that rise up against me: thou hast delivered me from the violent man. [49] Therefore will I give thanks unto thee, O Lord, among the heathen, and sing praises unto thy name. [50] Great deliverance giveth he to his king; and sheweth mercy to his anointed, to David, and to his seed forever."

As I said earlier, God wanted those words to be rooted and grounded in me. God had the same answer and message for me to reiterate in case doubt would increase or set precedence in my tests. 2 Samuel 22:1-51 says, "[1]And David spake unto the Lord the words of this song in the day that the Lord had delivered him out of the hand of all his enemies, and out of the hand of Saul: [2] And he said, The Lord is my rock, and my fortress, and my deliverer; [3] The God of my rock; in him will I trust: he is my shield, and the horn of my salvation, my high tower, and my refuge, my saviour; thou savest me from violence. [4] I will call on the Lord, who is worthy to be praised: so shall I be saved from mine enemies. [5] When the waves of death compassed me, the floods of ungodly men made me afraid; [6] The sorrows of hell compassed me about; the snares of death prevented me; [7] In my distress I called upon the Lord, and cried to my God: and he did hear my voice out of his temple, and my cry did enter into his ears. [8] Then the earth shook and trembled; the foundations of heaven moved and shook, because he was wroth. [9]

There went up a smoke out of his nostrils, and fire out of his mouth devoured: coals were kindled by it. [10] He bowed the heavens also, and came down; and darkness was under his feet. [11] And he rode upon a cherub, and did fly: and he was seen upon the wings of the wind. [12] And he made darkness pavilions round about him, dark waters, and thick clouds of the skies. [13] Through the brightness before him were coals of fire kindled. [14] The Lord thundered from heaven, and the most High uttered his voice. [15] And he sent out arrows, and scattered them; lightning, and discomfited them. [16] And the channels of the sea appeared, the foundations of the world were discovered, at the rebuking of the Lord, at the blast of the breath of his nostrils. [17] He sent from above, he took me; he drew me out of many waters; [18] He delivered me from my strong enemy, and from them that hated me: for they were too strong for me. [19] They prevented me in the day of my calamity: but the Lord was my stay. [20] He brought me forth also into a large place: he delivered me, because he delighted in me. [21] The Lord rewarded me according to my righteousness: according to the cleanness of my hands hath he recompensed me. [22] For I have kept the ways of the Lord, and have not wickedly departed from my God. [23] For all his judgments were before me: and as for his statutes, I did not depart from them. [24] I was also upright before him, and have kept myself from mine iniquity. [25] Therefore the Lord hath recompensed me according to my righteousness; according to my cleanness in his eye sight. [26] With the merciful thou wilt shew thyself merciful, and with the upright man thou wilt shew thyself upright. [27] With the pure thou wilt shew thyself pure; and with the froward thou wilt shew thyself unsavoury. [28] And the afflicted people thou wilt save: but thine eyes are upon the haughty, that thou mayest bring them down. [29] For thou art my lamp, O Lord: and the Lord will lighten my darkness. [30] For by thee I have run through a troop: by my God have I leaped over a wall. [31] As for God, his way is perfect; the word of the Lord is tried: he is a buckler to all them that trust in him. [32] For who is God, save the Lord? and who is a rock, save our God? [33] God is my strength and power: and he maketh my way perfect. [34] He maketh my feet like hinds' feet: and setteth me upon my high places. [35] He teacheth my hands to war; so that a bow of steel is broken by mine arms. [36] Thou hast also given me the shield of thy salvation: and thy gentleness hath made me great. [37] Thou hast enlarged my steps under me; so that my feet did not slip. [38] I have pursued mine enemies, and destroyed them; and turned not again until I had consumed them. [39] And I have consumed them, and wounded them, that they could not arise: yea, they are fallen under my feet. [40] For thou hast girded me with strength to battle: them that rose up against me hast thou subdued under me. [41] Thou hast also given me the necks of mine enemies, that I might destroy them that hate me. [42] They looked, but there was none to save; even unto the Lord, but he answered them not. [43] Then did I beat them as small as the dust of the earth, I did stamp them as the mire of the street, and did spread them abroad. [44] Thou also hast delivered me from the strivings of my people, thou hast kept me to be head of the heathen: a people which I knew not shall serve me. [45] Strangers shall submit themselves unto me: as soon as they hear, they shall be obedient unto me. [46] Strangers shall fade away, and they shall be afraid out of their close places. [47] The Lord liveth; and blessed be my rock; and exalted be the God of the rock of my salvation. [48] It is God that avengeth me, and that bringeth down the people under me. [49] And that bringeth me forth from mine enemies: thou also hast lifted me up on high above them that rose up against me: thou hast delivered me from the violent man. [50] Therefore I will give thanks unto thee, O Lord, among the heathen, and I will sing praises unto thy name. [51] He is the tower of salvation for his king: and sheweth mercy to his anointed, unto David, and to his seed for evermore."

✳✳✳

Therefore, Psalm 18:1-50 and 2 Samuel 22:1-51 are repeats of each other. When Jesus says, verily, verily or truly, truly in the New Testament, especially in John, it is Jesus's own original idea. Whenever Jesus says truly, truly or verily, verily, those are not just an opinion on the truth, those are intimate, personal first-hand knowledge. Same with these verses, Psalm 18:1-50 and 2 Samuel 22: 1-51, this is David's personal first-hand knowledge. He has experienced everything I have written in this book: the good, the bad, and the indifferent. This is not an idea or thought, but what I have experienced and gone through personally. My mess has become my message. My test is my testimony. You don't know the story behind my glory until you read this book. I can truly say when walking with God, you will become a "desert baby" where there is full dryness and lack of humidity. This is the time God wants you to come unto Him. Lay out before Him. Above all, sell out completely to Him. You will feel His presence. "Thou wilt shew me the path of life, in thy presence is fullness of joy, at the right hand there are pleasures for evermore." Psalm 16:11 The greatest expression of God's presence is in Jesus. Immanuel. God with us.

To have peace and joy is to have God's presence continually.

***

I remember when we were coming up as children. We could not go to sock hops, prom, high school dances on the weekend, football games, basketball games, and neither the out-of-town trips. The Lord did touch my mother's heart to allow me to be a girl scout and sing in the glee club, which is now called the gospel choir or regular show choir. I did get to spend two nights in the woods with the girl scouts in the 6th grade. Those were the kinder and gentler times in the mid-sixties. All those activities were taboo in our church and sure enough in our home. When I became a teacher, all those above activities still existed, except for the "sock hops," which is now called "the dance." The students now will say, "Are you going to the dance?" or "What are you going to wear to the dance?" or "Who are you going to the dance with?" The sock hop is a thing of the past.

In my career, being a high school teacher, we had all kinds of school sports and the teachers were expected to sponsor a team, sell tickets at the door, work the concession stand, or help chaperone the games. Well, I was trying to figure out where I would fit in. I said, "I know. I will work the concession stand and sell food." When I was young, we were taught going to the games was a sin. Then my principal spoke to us at the faculty meeting and said every teacher had to attend at least one home game and chaperone. I asked myself, "What am I going to do now?" A voice said to me softly, "You are not attending the game on your own accord. It is a mandate from your principal." So, I went on and signed my name for the game, and the night I would work. When I got there, the visiting team sat on the opposite side of the home team, as well as the cheerleaders. I did not see any sin in that.

The people were there laughing, hollering, and cheering on their team. I did not see the sin in that. They were drinking pops and eating popcorn and hot dogs. Some had candy, nachos, chips, etc. I did not see the sin in that. The opposite team would "boo" when the other team got points. Then, the teams would get points, and this went back and forth all night long until the time was up on the clock. I did not see the sin in that. They even had a break time which was called, "intermission." People would go to the restroom and revisit the concessions stand. I still did not see the sin in that. The cheerleaders would get out on the floor and cheer their team on. If I had to say, there was a little sin in that. The cheerleaders were dressed a little provocatively with their legs, thighs, and midriff exposed. That was not going to happen in my home. Not with my parent's three daughters. All my life I was always begging to be a majorette because of the size of my legs back then. Now being a majorette is a horse of another color. You are allowed to be any size or shape now because of non-discrimination, which is a blessing. I concluded, as an adult, that going to the game, is not a sin.

***

I had to chaperone a senior prom. I was well over 35 years old. I did not know what to expect, but I knew to dress formal or semi-formal. That mission was accomplished for me. I went to the prom as a teacher, sponsor, and chaperone. I wore a beautiful two-piece gold suit with rhinestone, gold pumps, gold shimmering hose, and hair all frozen up on my head with rhinestone jewelry. I looked pretty and felt pretty. Oh, those juniors and seniors were dressed to the nines in their formal attire and after-five frock. Girls had makeovers, hair extensions, nails, and toes manicured. They had beautiful jewelry and long eyelashes. They all looked like movie stars or they were ready for the runway. The gentlemen had on very sharp tuxedos, haircuts with all kinds of sketches, suede skin shoes; some had rhinestone shoes, fancy cartoon character vests with beautiful bowties, and very fancy jewelry. These guys were all ready for the runway as well. They danced a little, took a lot of pictures, and ate very little food because some had already gone to dinner before they got there. Then little by little, limousines would arrive out front and pick up multiple couples and that was the end of that. Most students had their own cars, parent's cars, or sibling's cars. They would start leaving as well. Some would rent hotel rooms and have smaller "after parties." Some would spend the night at the hotel, and a few went home. Nevertheless, it was clean fun. It was a time for seniors to spend their last dance with each other in formal attire. I did not see anything wrong with that. Maybe what they did after the prom may have been questionable.

***

The out-of-town trips I would take with my students during the Spring Breaks would be so much fun and joy. We would mostly go to New York for nine days. We would take the 19-hour ride from Memphis to Manhattan, New York on a bus with TV screens throughout the bus and watch movie after movie. Then we would fall asleep, wake up and eat, and watch more movies that would be playing in the theaters. We would stop and get a real wholesome meal at a reputable restaurant that was well frequented by tourists. We would visit each other on the bus. Some students would come and sit with me for hours on end.

Since I would always have a group of 30 or more, they would meet me in the conference room for free at the hotel. We would all meet at a certain time and have a talent show. You had the opportunity to sing, rap, dance, do a poem, or whatever you wanted to present. It was fine with me, as long as it was clean. We would always have winners in either 1st place, 2nd place, and 3rd place. The students wanted me to judge because I was over the senior class and talent shows. We would stay in the conference room until I got them real sleepy. We would leave there and everybody would be tired, sleepy, and worn out. God would bless all my trips to be a success. No fighting, no one was disrespectful, and everybody had their own money. Hallelujah, Thank you, Jesus!

Before we left the city, I would give the students who traveled with me a big drill and spin about their money. I told them to keep their money on them at all times including when they are sleeping, looking at TV, or even in the restroom. And to not trust anyone with their money or to watch their money. I told them if their money comes up missing, do not tell me. There is nothing I can do because it is their word against the other. Students will lie about bringing a large sum of money and only brought two hundred dollars. Some parents would wire money there for their children. Parents would overnight it because some parents would not have gotten paid until after we left for New York. Those students would carry to New York anywhere from $200 to $1000. Once we would make it to Canale Street and Malcolm Shabazz Avenue, they would be on cloud nine because they were able to get all the designer things and latest fashions for knock-off prices. Even though they were knock-offs, they were so happy to wheel and deal with the people and the people would give them double discounts because they were from Memphis and because they were children.

I did this for about 15-20 years. The world had begun to change and above all, children began to change. I knew I had come to the end of the road. My principal would send me out-of-town on the day trips with the student council. I was very much satisfied. I had reached that plateau in traveling with students. I was fulfilled, not having the exposure as a student myself. God gave me the victory and the exposure in this life while I was clothed in my right mind. This worked well with me and for me because I did not have children of my own and my husband was not with me. Everything I went through in my life and career, God graced me for it. I read this, and I would like to share this with you.

I left work early so I could have some uninterrupted study time right before the final in my Youth Issues class. When I got to class, everybody was doing their last minute studying. The teacher came in and said he would review with us for just a little bit before the test. We went through the review, most of it right on the study guide, but there were some things he was reviewing that I had never heard of. When questioned about it, he said that they were in the book and we were responsible for everything in the book. We couldn't really argue with that.

Finally, it was time to take the test. "Leave them face down on the desk until everyone has one and I'll tell you to start," our professor instructed. When we turned them over, every answer on the test was filled in! The bottom of the last page said the following:

"This is the end of the Final Exam. All the answers on your test are correct. You will receive an 'A' on the final exam. The reason you passed the test is because the creator of the test took it for you. All the work you did in preparation for this test did not help you get the A. You have just experienced...grace." He then went around the room and asked each student individually, "What is your grade? Do you deserve the grade you are receiving? How much did all your studying for this exam help you achieve your final grade?"

Now I am not a crier by any stretch of the imagination, but I had to fight back tears when answering those questions and thinking about how the Creator has passed the test for me.

Discussion afterward went like this: "I have tried to teach you all semester that you are a recipient of grace. I've tried to communicate to you that you need to demonstrate this gift as you work with young people.

Don't hammer them; they are not the enemy. Help them, for they will carry on your ministry if it is full of GRACE!"

Talking about how some of us had probably studied hours and some just a few minutes, but had all received the same grade, he pointed to a story Jesus told in Matthew 20. The owner of a vineyard hired people to work in his field and agreed to pay them a certain amount. Several different times during the day, he hired more workers. When it was time to pay them, they all received the same amount. When the ones who had been hired first thing in the morning began complaining, the boss said, "Should you be angry because I am kind?" (Matthew 20:15).

The teacher said he had never done this kind of final before and probably would never do it again, but because of the content of many of our class discussions, he felt like we needed to experience grace.

Have you thanked your Creator today because of the grace you have experienced?' (Experiencing Grace, Denise Banderman, 2002)

I thank God for passing the test for me and carrying me when I could not carry myself. It is a joy to experience Grace. It is unmerited favor. Now that I'm older, I can look back and see that it was Grace that has brought me this far. Grace and Favor are better than money. You can have all the money in the world, but you cannot buy Grace. When you walk with the Lord, and talk with Him, He becomes the center of your joy and the head of your life.

***

When we were coming up, in our denomination, they really had a lot of no's. Our denomination could have been named the "'No' Denomination." Everything we wanted to do or go to, the answer was just plain, No. We knew not to demand a reason or a why. When our parents and church leaders told us, "No," it was concrete and etched in stone. There were no ifs, ands, or buts about it. Can we go to the movies? No. Can we go skating? No. Can we wear makeup? No. Can we have a friend of the opposite sex? No. No. No. Can we spend the night over one of our friend's house? No. No. Can we hang out at the mall? No. No. No. Can we cut our hair? No. Can we wear miniskirts? No. Can we wear hot pants? No. No. No. We could wear pedal pushers, capri pants, bell bottoms, hip huggers, or just plain pants. Ever now and then we could sneak and wear palazzo pants because they looked like a wide-legged skirt if you did not walk wide-legged and the split was not obvious between both legs. Later on in life, our parents would always quote Deuteronomy 22:5, "The woman shall not wear that which pertaineth unto a man, neither shall a man put on a woman's garment for all that do so are abomination unto the Lord thy God."

Moses said to Israel: Women must not pretend to be men, and men must not pretend to be women. The Lord your God is disgusted with people who do that. The basic principle presented in the above scripture is that males and females are to honor the dignity of their own sex and not to attempt to adopt the appearance or role of their opposite sex. God never makes a mistake. Whatever your gender was at birth, it should be the same at death. You have gone beyond God when you decide to do a sex change for you or your child. Woe be unto you. Reckoning day is coming, like it will be for any other sin, big or small. The scripture above clearly forbids transvestism, which is a deviant form of sexual behavior. That is why it is so important to read the Bible for yourself and run references. "Wisdom is the principal thing therefore get wisdom: and with all thy getting get an understanding." Proverbs 4:7

For years, children at school and even my peers would ask me eagerly why I did not do certain things or wear certain things. I would tell them thoughtlessly, "Because my mother said so." Now that I am older, people are not going on opinions, beliefs, or traditions. There is no validity behind that. I was not reading the Word for myself, so therefore I would say, "My mama said so." But what does the Word say? "Heaven and earth shall pass away, but my words shall not pass away." Matthew 24:35 "In the beginning was the Word, and the Word was with God, and the Word was God. The same was in the beginning with God." John 1:1-2 "This have ye made the commandment of God no effect by your tradition." Matthew 15:6b "But in vain they do worship me, teaching for the doctrines, the commandments of men." Matthew 15:9

My mom's opinions and beliefs did not have a true foundation but she was teaching us to the best of her ability. I can truly say, because of the love and sincerity she had for God, God knew her heart, and He rewarded her, in her lack of understanding. I can truly say, my mother's teaching kept us from a million failures. It was better to err on the side of caution. Today we know better. We know to read and reread the "Word of God." I always tell new beginners to start in Psalm and let God lead them from there. God's word is a true foundation. "The grass withers, the flower fades, but word of God stands forever." Isaiah 40:8

So when anyone asks me anything about life or religion, I use the Word as my foundation and do all I can to point them to Jesus. He is the only One that can save them and keep them in this untoward and perverse generation. Living for God is a made-up mind. God will keep you if you want to be kept. The Bible says that God blessed Caleb because he had a different spirit or a different attitude than the rest of the people. In Numbers 14:24, Caleb remained wholeheartedly loyal to God. Caleb followed God when no one else did, and his uncompromising obedience earned him a lasting reward.

There are many rewards for faithfulness to the Lord. According to Job 14:1, we will not be able to escape trouble, because we are man, born of a woman, and these days are full of trouble. God will see to it that trouble turns into triumph and that all things will work out for our good. Then the Bible speaks about Noah walking with

God. "Noah was a just man and perfect in his generations, and Noah walked with God." Genesis 6:9b

It is very important to walk with God because it assures us of his presence and power in our lives. It also means that we are in agreement with God about our life. "Can two walk together, except they be agreed?" Amos 3:3 Walking with God means you are in agreement with Him and His ways. No one is perfect, but when you are walking with God, your desire should be to see your own selfish desires die for the sake of seeing God transform you more and more in the image of His Son. "Therefore if any many be in Christ, he is a new creature: old things are passed away, behold, all things become new." 2 Corinthians 5:17

***

I thank God for the 50 years I lived in the south part of the inner city, and when my husband married me, we moved to Davis Tower, overlooking the river. Even though I lived downtown, I was still living in the southern part of the inner city. I never dreamed or thought about going any further than East Memphis off of the Poplar Avenue and Massey area, or maybe the middle leg of Kirby Parkway. I never dreamed of living in the suburbs; I just thought that life was above me and out of my reach. I know now, that with God, all things are possible.

Since living in my home, there was one time when my sister came to visit me, and I asked her if I could borrow $700. She gladly gave me the money and told me not to worry about paying it back. She said she just wanted to be able to help in any way she could. She was able to help me with incidentals in my new home. My God saw me through everything and gave me the Victory with His Right Hand and Holy Arm.

I never shared with any of my family members the struggles I faced during the years. It would have been the 'Talk of the Nation,' which would have ridiculed me for making the purchase of this home based on my financial position and teaching salary. But, I was reminded of God's Word and promise that says "In quietness and confidence shall be your strength." And boy did I ever grab that truth by the horns and live it to the fullness of God. My siblings would have asked me, what must have I been thinking, who was I trying to impress, or why would I do something so irrational? And even though my family knew I always had favor upon my life, they would have told me I didn't need more favor, I needed a Miracle from Heaven and should be locked inside the church forever to maintain this home on a lake and behind a gate.

I knew this had to be a Faith Walk, and when trusting God for something truly extraordinary, you can talk to Him, and He will direct you to the people needing to hear your testimony. It was this test that inspired me to pray more, fast more, trust more, and read more of his Word. God did not change my situation but my situation Changed Me. "But God. Won't He do it?" 15 years later, I am still living in my Golf Course, Gated Community Dream House on the Lake.

The Lord has spoken and said He has something even better in store for me. My brother told me that many Pastors and Bishops weren't living the life I was. Our test draws us closer to God and helps us learn more of Him. "Take my yoke upon you, and learn from me, for I am gentle and humble in heart, and you will find rest in your souls. For my yoke is easy, and my burden is light" Matthew 11:29-30 Jesus's yoke is never forced on us because He is a gentleman. We all have to decide to put on the yoke. That is why Jesus tells us to 'Take my yoke' and we must be willing to receive it by surrendering our will to His will. By doing this, it equips us to resist temptations and to extend our understanding of God. Your test will really help you to draw near to God. He is the only one that can cool the flames that lighten the load.

Since I was married, I lived and still living a celibate life. Different males have approached from different facets. Some came with finances and prosperity. Some came through physical appearance and were very easy on the eye. Some came through business. Some came through social life and some played the romance card. My testimony was and is, "I will never let go of God's hands." They did not have enough of anything to buy the God out of my life. The human part of me was tempted and flattered. Satan will always send you counterfeits when you are headed toward your destiny. I knew to stay and keep my eyes on the Lord. That is why it is so good to read the Word and memorize it. The Devil or Satan knows exactly what he sends. You know in life it is easy to get rid of something you do not like. If you like a tall, dark, medium-sized man with a beautiful smile, Satan is not going to send you a short, light, skinny man with a smile that needs dental work done. That is easy to walk away from. Whenever Satan presents something as good, because he is cunning, it will always go against humanity and God.

Always stay prayerful and watchful. "Be sober, be vigilant, because your adversary the devil as a roaring lion, walketh about, seeking whom he may devour." I Peter 5:8 I thank God for my parents teaching us the Word at a young age. "My soul shall be satisfied as with marrow and fatness, and my mouth shall praise thee with joyful lips." Psalm 63:5 My parents reared us up, pointing us to Jesus.

Today, we are at His feet. Being at Jesus's feet allows us to hear from God. It shows that we recognize who He is, and it shows how much we trust Him and believe Him. Going through deserts teaches me more about God than going through green pastures. The three Hebrew boys in the Bible, Shadrach, Meshach, and Abednego knew of God through their beliefs and teachings. That is why they could say with confidence, "O Nebuchadnezzar, we are not careful to answer thee in this matter. If it be so, our God whom we serve is able to deliver us from the burning fiery furnace, and he will deliver us out of thine hand, O King. But if not, be it known unto thee, O king, that we will not serve thy gods, nor worship the golden image which thou hast set up." Daniel 3:16b-18

Now the three Hebrew boys' words and faith were tested just as we are going to be tested by Satan for being ambassadors and living epistles for Christ. "And he commanded the most mighty men that were in his army to bind Shadrach, Meshach, and Abednego, and to cast them into the burning fiery furnace." Daniel 3:20 "And these three men, Shadrach, Meshach, and Abednego, fell down bound into the midst of the burning fiery furnace. Then Nebuchadnezzar the king was astonished, and rose up in haste, and spake, and said unto his counsellors, Did not we cast three men bound into the midst of the fire? They answered and said unto the king, True, O king. He answered and said, Lo, I see four men loose, walking in the midst of the fire, and they have no hurt; and the form of the fourth is like the Son of God." Daniel 3:23-25

The three Hebrew boys had no hurt because God had gotten in the fire with them and cooled the flames. They were tested by their faith. "But the just shall live by his faith." Habakkuk 2:4 "For therein is the righteousness of God revealed from faith to faith: as it is written, The just shall live by faith." Romans 1:17 Daniel in the Bible was thrown in the Lion's Den because he refused to give credence to the decree: *no one should worship no other God for 30 days, but to King Darius.*

The Bible says this when Daniel knew the decree was signed. "Now when Daniel knew that the writing was signed, he went into the house, and his windows being opened to his chamber toward Jerusalem, he kneeled upon his knees three time a day, and prayed, and gave thanks, before his God as he did aforetime." Daniel 6:10 "Then answered they and said before the king, That Daniel, which is of the children of the captivity of Judah, regardeth not thee, O king, nor the decree that thou hast signed, but maketh his petition three times a day." Daniel 6:13 "Then the king arose very early in the morning, and went in haste unto the den of lions. And when he came to the den, he cried with a lamentable voice unto Daniel: and the king spake and said to Daniel, O Daniel, servant of the living God, is thy God, whom thou servest continually, able to deliver thee from the lions? Then said Daniel unto the king, O king, live for ever. My God hath sent his angel, and hath shut the lions' mouths, that they have not hurt me: forasmuch as before him innocency was found in me; and also before thee, O king, have I done no hurt. The king was overjoyed and gave orders to lift Daniel out of the den.

And when Daniel was lifted from the den, no wound was found on him, because he had trusted in his God." Daniel 6:19-23

"And the king commanded, and they brought those men which had accused Daniel, and they cast them into the den of lions, them, their children, and their wives; and the lions had the mastery of them, and brake all their bones in pieces or ever they came at the bottom of the den. Then King Darius wrote unto all people, nations, and languages, that dwell in all the earth; Peace be multiplied unto you. I make a decree, That in every dominion of my kingdom men tremble and fear before the God of Daniel: for he is the living God, and stedfast for ever, and his kingdom that which shall not be destroyed, and his dominion shall be even unto the end. He delivereth and rescueth, and he worketh signs and wonders in heaven and in earth, who hath delivered Daniel from the power of the lions. So this Daniel prospered in the reign of Darius, and in the reign of Cyrus the Persian." Daniel 6:24-28

I remember seeing a picture in a book where Daniel was lying back on a lion for his pillow, reading the Bible. The Lord had gotten in the den with Daniel as He did with the Hebrew boys in the fiery furnace. Once God gets under our load, we can make it and face anything that tomorrow holds. Their faith was tested, but they trusted in God. Job said, "Though you slay me, yet will I trust you." Job's ending was better than his beginning. God gave Job double for his trouble. Whatever we go through, whatever betide us, God will take care of us. Our good days will always outweigh our bad days. We cannot complain. God will never let go of our hands. God will never leave us. If there is separation because we left God or we took our hand out of His hand, God will never leave us alone.

I have experienced that for myself during the vicissitudes of life. During my wilderness experiences, valley experiences, and my lonely hours, it was God that was carrying me because I did not have the strength to stand up and carry myself. God was also under the load. As the old adage says, "Experience is the Best Teacher." Once you walk with God during the dark times in your life, you do not want to let go of His hand. With God's right hand and holy arm, you will have the victory. "O sing unto the LORD a new song; for he hath done marvellous things: his right hand, and his holy arm, hath gotten him the victory." Psalm 98:1

***

You read how I like to drive Cadillacs. I thank God that I was able to drive Cadillacs for over 34 years. As I mentioned earlier, God gave me favor with the owner. I was able to drive any style and any color. It would have vogue tires, fancy rims, and sunroof tops. Sometimes it would have double sunroofs, special designer grills, and ragtops. I did not have to make a down payment or do a trade-in or closing fee. I would just pick out the car, tell them the car note range I was comfortable with, and then drive off into the sunset. God did that. I would flip every three years, or sometimes every two. I would have the fanciest and prettiest Cadillac in the city. They had a TV show called, "Pimp My Ride." Please forgive me, but all my rides were pimped. You can tell I taught school because I learned their lingo, culture, and style. It was fun. They knew regardless of what, in the midst of, because of, that I Loved the Lord with all my heart and soul. That was my first priority, main priority, and all in between priority. They knew I had a toe hold on the Word and was righteous. "Righteousness exalts a nation, but sin is a reproach to any people." Proverbs 14:34

As I close the chapters to my book and begin to end my testimonies, if I had to sum up this entire book in three words, I would say that "Prayer Changes Things." Be consistent. Be instant about it. Be diligent and watch God turn your life around. "The grass withereth, the flower fadeth, but the Word of God shall stand forever." Isaiah 40:8 "He which testifieth these things saith, Surely come quickly. Amen. Even so, come, Lord Jesus." Revelation 22:20

Continued Testimonies

It was right after Christmas, four days to be exact. It was December 29, 2004. There were about five or six ladies who met at my parent's home. One of the five was going to purchase a piece of exercise equipment from my dad, and the others were going to join in prayer for my mom and dad. God is omniscient. He knows everything. So, the leader of the prayer prayed for everyone in the house, except for my dad. I was hoping and praying before she left, she would pray for my dad, too. Well, she didn't. Nothing happens unless the Lord allows it. They went home, and I went home. Later that night, I received a phone call that my dad had gotten very sick and wanted to go to the hospital by ambulance. I lived 15 minutes away. I went to be with my mom that night, December 29th, not knowing that would be the beginning of a new chapter in my life.

My dad was in the hospital, and my mom and I went every day after I left work. They ran several tests on him and could not find anything. I had to get up early each morning at 5:00 a.m., get my mom dressed to take her to my dad's sister's home, and would leave there running, trying to make it to work on time by 7:15 a.m. Then, I would get my mother each evening, and we would go to the hospital. We did this routine for about seven to nine days. When we would visit him, he seemed so distant. He told us not to come back and that he was doing good and just wanted to sleep. He told us emphatically to go home. My other siblings had gone to visit him as well. They said he was very distant with them, and they could tell he was transitioning from Earth to Glory. They saw it but just did not want to receive it. I asked my dad that evening how he was doing. He told me, "When I came in my back was hurting and now the pain has gone." He began to raise both legs and arms and told me he did not have pain anywhere. As he told me that, the Lord told me these words, "Many are the afflictions of the righteous, but the Lord delivereth him out of them all." Psalm 34:19

That word was manifested right before me and that was marvelous in my eyes. My dad did not make it back home. He had called and told my sister that he did not want to go back home. It was hard for my dad to deal with and live with my mom having dementia. They had been married for 61 years, and she was every bit, as the Word says. "his help meet." My dad really loved and respected my mom's decisions and some of her choices. He was 78 years old, and he was in denial concerning her condition. Even though her dementia was prevalent and noticeable, he never gave credence to the fact that she had it. Therefore, he was an unhappy man seeing her change, but not accepting the change. So God gave my dad the desire of his heart and gave him his mansion in heaven.

"In my Father's house are many mansions: if it were not so, I would have told you. I go to prepare a place for you. And if I go and prepare a place for you, I will come again, and receive you unto myself; that where I am, there ye may be also. And whither I go ye know, and the way ye know. Thomas saith unto him, LORD, we know not whither thou goest; and how can we know the way? Jesus saith unto him, I am the way, the truth, and the life: no man cometh unto the Father, but by me." John 14:2-6

My mom and I went every evening as I stated earlier, but the Friday before his departure, I told my mother I was too tired to go to the hospital. I told her when I picked her up from my dad's sister's home, that we would go home instead, get a good night's rest, and go to the hospital on Saturday morning and stay all day. I was worn to a frazzle. Getting up every morning in the wee hours, dressing her, feeding her, taking her to midtown, and then going to work pass downtown. It was exhausting teaching my students, more than 180 minds a day, with my one mind. My mom and I got up that Saturday, following the plan that we had scheduled. As we were getting ready to walk out, my brother called breathing very hard in the phone like he had run a marathon; he said, "Daddy is gone." I kept saying, "For real?" I would say it every time he repeated it. I gasped real loud and told my mom what he said. With my mom being in the state of dementia, she probably thought I meant, he had just left home. Nevertheless, she showed no emotions. My family members, some of our church members, and my estranged husband, all met at the hospital where he had transitioned. My sister had boarded a plane and was on her way.

The chaplain came in to pray and counsel us. He began to look around and said, "Well I can look at each of you and tell you all have a relationship with God already and you do not need me." He left the room. We heard a loud howling sound from down the hall. We had no idea who that was or what that was. It was my poor husband howling like he had lost everybody in his family. He needed a physician, a bed, a chaplain, and needed to be sedated. He was weeping and wailing. It seems as if he took away all our pain and bottled it up in his body. He was a pitiful man. I knew he loved my dad, but not like that. *How could he have walked away from my dad's daughter, me?* It could have been guilt. It could have been that he wanted to apologize. I don't know, but I do know the Bible says to live each day like it is your last day, centered around Psalm 90:12.

We buried my father the following Saturday. We'd purchased a beautiful mausoleum for him and my mother, and put them in the high-end cemetery in Memphis. My father had really invested in us, so we reciprocated big time in return. My father was also a Cadillac man. We sent him to his heavenly home, Cadillac style. He had enough flowers to decorate or cover a half-mile. "Lo, I am with you always, even unto the end of the world." Matthew 28:20b The Lord was with my father from earth to glory. I never had any biological children, but when my father passed on to Glory, I became a mother to my mother instantaneously. No one told me to do it. No one asked me to do it. God just transitioned it to me immediately. I was glad to do it. It was an honor to do it. God was with me every step of the way. My mother was a widow. A widow indeed. "Honour widows that are widows indeed. But if any widow have children or nephews, let them learn first to shew piety at home, and to requite their parents: for that is good and acceptable before God. Now she that is a widow indeed, and desolate, trusteth in God, and continueth in supplications and prayers night and day. But if any provide not for his own, and specially for those of his own house, he hath denied the faith, and is worse than an infidel. Let not a widow be taken into the number under threescore years old, having been the wife of one man. Well reported of for good works; if she have brought up children, if she have lodged strangers, if she have washed the saints' feet, if she have relieved the afflicted, if she have diligently followed every good work. If any man or woman that believeth have widows, let them relieve them, and let not the church be charged; that it may relieve them that are widows indeed." 1 Timothy 5:3-5, 8-10, 16

I gave my mom another whole life. She had lost a lot of weight and became two to three inches shorter. I bought her a new wardrobe. Our caregiver picked out beautiful short wigs. We kept her with pearls on, pearl earrings, and bracelets. I went and purchased her a full-length mink because mostly everywhere I went, I wore one of my minks. I wanted my mom to look like me, every step of the way. We put makeup on her. The caregiver would dress her first. She would sit her by the front door, and my mom would cross her knees over each other because she knew special attention was being given to her. You could look at her and tell she felt pretty. I would fly her across the country to visit her favorite relatives. She was taken out to dinner two to three times a week. We did not, and I especially did not, want her to desire anything. I did my level best to make my mom happy. I would fix her up every Saturday and carry her to the Wolfchase Mall, and we would sit down in the food court and watch the passing parade.

I treated her like I would have wanted to be treated. I treated her with respect and dignity, even though she was battling dementia and the loss of her husband of 61 years. I had to make every decision for her. I would feed her, bathe her, dress her, get her hair professionally done, and all the other nine yards. It was a struggle after working with 180 students a day, but that was my mother. Some days she would act like a child. I would give her food, and she would turn it completely over. I would put clothes on her, and as soon as I turned my back to get something for her, she would have taken them all off. I knew what my mother would do, so I would get up an extra two hours earlier to be ahead of the mishaps, incidents, or accidents. I did this week after week, month after month, until finally, I left school one Friday evening. It seemed as if I could not take it anymore. I climbed up in my truck and screamed to the top of my voice these words, "GOD, I HURT", and the tears streamed down my face like a river.

I would carry my mom to church and sit in the back with her with tears streaming down. I was at my wit's end. I got up one morning and turned on the TV. It was like God had that commercial for me. It was about how to get help with your loved ones who are seniors. God opened that door wide for me. The people came to my job the next day, explained the program to me, let me sign the papers, and the lady started working immediately. She was a true caregiver and idealistic. God hand-picked her, even though she had a dark side to her that we did not know about. However, she still was idealistic. My entire family approved of her.

Finally, maybe two years later, she quit. So many things were happening to her and her children until she felt condemned and cursed. Nevertheless, she did an impeccable job with my mom's home and my mom. God will always take care of his own. My mother was not able to talk or express herself about anything that went on. God was my mother's stay.

***

My elder sister has always been blessed with favor upon her life, and she has been away from home for 50 years. She graduated from college and bought her a spanking brand new car without working one day. She just showed the car company that she had a contract to become a teacher. In regards to that hand-typed paper, they gave her a brand new car of her choice. That really made my dad happy and encouraged all of us to go to college, and we all did, even the grandchildren. All three of her children are engineers. Her elder daughter opened up a Hyundai dealership and got her training over in Lebanon. She was one of the top people for the company in Montgomery. Her two other children are successful engineers with the perks of the company. She brought her children up in prayer and Bible study, even though they did not appreciate it then. Her children and grandchildren are very comfortable. "All your children shall be taught by the Lord, and great shall be the peace of your children." Isaiah 54:13

My sister invested so many years and hours into teaching other children the scriptures in the Bible, biblical plays, and shut-ins in church. She would always give out money to children who would learn different scriptures and different parts of the Bible. She invested in the youth, and God has blessed her seeds and is working things out for them. If you take care of God's business, what concerns you, concerns God as well. "The righteous who walks in his integrity, blessed are his children after Him." Proverbs 20:7 "Cast thy bread upon the waters; for thou shalt find it after many days." Ecclesiastes 11:1

To summarize my book, it talks about uncertainties, transitions and transitionings, shifting, changes, instability, unpredictability, reversals, alterations, hardships, diversity, difficulties, and pandemonium. Everything in life has pros and cons and ups and downs. For the most part, we see all as troubles, but it is really answers to prayers disguised as trouble. It is similar to being sick and the doctor gives you a shot. It doesn't feel good, but it is good for your good. Even some medicines we take doesn't taste good and might have some side effects, but it turns out to be for our wellness.

Prayer is the key to everything and faith unlocks the door. It is impossible to please God without faith. You have seen how having an active prayer life early in the morning was essential.

"The grass withereth, the flower fadeth: but the word of our God shall stand for ever." Isaiah 40:8 "The Lord watch between me and thee, when we are absent one from another." Genesis 31:49 "He which testifieth these things saith, Surely I come quickly. Amen. Even so, come, LORD Jesus." Revelation 22:20

About The Author

Dr. Aretha Coleman-Terry was born in Memphis, TN. She is a retired math teacher who served in this career for 35 years. As a teacher, Dr. Coleman-Terry was able to not only teach her students about math, but she ministered to them spiritually as well. She is also a passionate advocate for children. She has done missionary work since her walk with Christ and has been a minister for 14 years and an ordained Elder for four years. She has traveled to 12 countries, building schools, starting churches, and "Lifting Up Jesus" in Beijing, China on top of the ground and not underground. To God Be The Glory for the opened door. Last but not least, she is a philanthropist who gives from her heart and to meet the needs of others. Her motto is Always smiling with J.O.Y.

(**J**esus first, **O**thers second, and **Y**ourself last.)
This is free.